Performance and Cure

CLASSICAL INTER/FACES SERIES
Edited by Susanna Braund and Paul Cartledge

PERFORMANCE AND CURE

Drama and Healing in
Ancient Greece
and Contemporary America

Karelisa V. Hartigan

Duckworth

First published in 2009 by
Gerald Duckworth & Co. Ltd.
90-93 Cowcross Street, London EC1M 6BF
Tel: 020 7490 7300
Fax: 020 7490 0080
info@duckworth-publishers.co.uk
www.ducknet.co.uk

A catalogue record for this book is available
from the British Library

ISBN 978 0 7156 3639 8

Typeset by Ray Davies
Printed and bound in Great Britain by
J F Print Ltd, Sparkford, Somerset

Contents

Preface

I was standing in the Asklepieion at ancient Pergamon, having just visited the city's magnificent theatre. I walked into the well-preserved *odeion* in the healing sanctuary and suddenly asked myself: 'Why is this here?' Then I thought about the other sites I had visited where theatres or another viewing space formed part of a sanctuary dedicated to Asklepios. And once again I asked myself, 'Why?' Thus began this study and here I present my answers.

Theatres stand in or adjacent to the majority of the ancient sanctuaries dedicated to Asklepios, god of healing. The archaeological evidence prompts the question: why did the Greeks construct theatres as a part of a healing sanctuary? Furthermore why, in Athens, was the new home for the cult of Asklepios placed immediately beside the theatre of Dionysos on the south slope of the Akropolis? Neither tragedy nor comedy was created for entertainment but to honour the god Dionysos. The Greeks did not build these theatres so that drama could be offered to divert and amuse those who came to the healing sanctuary with the sick. The performance space must have had some role in the rites performed for Asklepios.

To date, no one has asked the question why the Greeks considered a theatre to be a necessary part of an Asklepieion. Archaeologists have noted the presence of the theatre and its properties but have not discussed its purpose. Philologists study the texts of the plays performed in honour of Dionysos in the various city theatres but have not paid attention to those within healing sanctuaries (other than at Epidauros). They have not pondered what other dramatic use might be made of a theatre, such as that at Athens or Peiraeus; it is known, of course, that some public meetings were held in these convenient venues. If classical scholars consider medical terms and drama, they focus on how these terms are used within the texts, on how the ancient playwrights used words or metaphors from medicine as they do, for example, from sports. My study unites the two realms of archaeology, the physical presence of the performance space, and of drama, what went on in that space. From presentations of my work at conferences of professionals in the areas of classics, theatre, performance, ancient medicine, and the healing arts, I have learned that the idea is one in which there is great interest.

To begin my study, I examined evidence from both inscriptions and literary sources. These indicate that some type of dramatic perform-ance was a part of the rituals performed for the god. Several inscriptions from these Asklepieia record that a portion of the sacrificial offering is to be distributed to 'the members of the cho-rus'. While the main task of these choristers was to sing hymns in honour of the god, they may well have had further duties. Did they take part in plays staged for therapeutic reasons? This book sug-gests that ambulatory patients came to the theatre to assist in their recovery. The fact that at Pergamon there is an underground pas-sage between the *odeion* and the patients' sleeping hall (the *abaton*) strengthens the suggestion.

Epidauros was the most famous healing sanctuary in ancient Greece and the one from which other Asklepieia were established. Today the theatre at Epidauros remains the best preserved in Greece, still used for festival performances of drama every summer. But Epidauros is just one healing site with a theatre. There were over 300 sanctuaries dedicated to Asklepios throughout the Greek world, and of those with some archaeological remains extant, a theatre, large or small, forms part of the site. At Pergamon, a city in northwest Turkey centred around a magnificent theatre, a small *odeion* stands within the extensive sanctuary to Asklepios. At Dion in northern Greece, where again a fine theatre forms part of the main city, there is a small theatre within the god's cult area. At Oropos, a small city north of Athens on what was once the border between Attica and Boiotia, the Amphiaraion is adorned with an attractive little theatre adjacent to the stoa where the sick awaited the healing ministrations of the healing divinity. One of the major identifying structures at Messene in the western Peloponnese is the theatre within the sanctuary to Asklepios. And the list could go on. Finally, the site of the Asklepieion in Athens is worthy of consideration. When the healing god was brought to Athens, he needed a home, and a place for his cult was established immediately adjacent to the theatre of Dionysos on the south slope of the Akropolis. I believe that the placement was not a random choice.

Within the past several decades, the idea that medicine and art, especially dramatic art, can work together in the healing process has attracted the interest of medical professionals. Recent research stresses the connection between mind and body, between attitude and healing. Many doctors now understand the bond between art and medicine, and realize that this bond is not a recent discovery, that the roots of this concept lay with the ancient Greeks and the theatres they constructed at the sanctuaries dedicated to Asklepios.

In this book I present how dramatic art was linked to healing in the ancient world and how the two, art and medicine, work together in a contemporary hospital. I discuss how drama performed for patients was part of the ritual enacted at the ancient Asklepieia and how and why it assists in the healing process for the modern patient. The penultimate chapter provides evidence for the latter as I present my experiences as an actress in the Arts-in-Medicine program at Shands Hospital at the University of Florida. In a concluding section, I note that the adage that 'holy sites remain holy' applies especially to the sites once holy to Asklepios. For while a church or a chapel was frequently built within or adjacent to a ruined temple of many an ancient deity, at the sanctuaries of Asklepios there is deeper evidence of the continuity. Churches dedicated to the Saints Kosmas and Damian, saints whose legend and icons are reputed to have healing qualities, were constructed at the sites once sacred to the healing god. Within these churches the iconostasis is hung with *tamata* replicating the various body parts that they have healed, a direct repetition of the clay votive offerings hung up within the sanctuaries of Asklepios.

Acknowledgments

To the scholars who preceded me:
During the course of this study, I have found several books to be invaluable, texts without which I could not have undertaken or completed my book. For my investigation of Asklepios in the ancient world, the first work that requires special acknowledgement is the two-volumes-in-one study by Emma J. and Ludwig Edelstein, *Asclepius: Collection and Interpretation of the Testimonies*. This *mag-*

num opus collects in Volume I all known references to the god, his cult, and his sanctuaries, and offers full interpretation of these in Volume II. In second place stand the two exhaustive studies of Sara Aleshire: *The Athenian Asklepieion: The People, Their Dedications, and the Inventories* and *Asklepios at Athens: Epigraphic and Prosopographic Essays on the Athenian Healing Cults*. For the identification and location of the many cults of Asklepios, I am indebted to the work of Alessandra Semeria, 'Per un Censimento degli Asklepieia della Grecia Continentale e delle Isole', *ASNP* 16 (1986). Finally, the best general study, from which I culled many points, is the book by Louise Wells, *The Greek Language of Healing from Homer to New Testament Times*. References to these texts appear frequently in my pages.

For the modern interface, again several works stand out. For the link between the brain and healing, Paul Martin's study *The Healing Mind: The Vital Links Between Brain and Behavior, Immunity and Disease* stands first for inspiring me to pursue this avenue more fully. For the power of belief, among many studies that of Jerome and Julia Frank, *Persuasion and Healing: A Comparative Study of Psychotherapy*, was important. Guenter B. Risse wrote on the interface of the ancient and the modern in his extensive study, *Mending Bodies, Saving Souls: A History of Hospitals*, and I found much of value in his text. Two of the best books on the importance of the interaction between doctor and patient are those by Peter Berczeller: *Doctors and Patients* and Bernard Lown: *The Lost Art of Healing: Practicing Compassion in Medicine*. Although there are not many quotations from these doctors in my pages, their ideas lie behind many of my words. Finally, for the background on the material reported from my work as an actress at Shands Hospital, I first acknowledge Jonathan Fox for the concept of Playback Theatre. Secondly and most important, I recognize the vision of Dr John Graham-Pole. His book *Illness and the Art of Creative Self-Expression* and his several articles outline the importance of art in the healing process, and his establishment of the Arts-in-Medicine program at the University of Florida's hospital made my work there possible.

To the colleagues, friends, and family who supported me:
This is the moment in a book when the author tries to recall all those who touched her life as she worked on the text. As usual, there are too

many to name, and probably many whose influence was not recognized at the time. But several people must be acknowledged and I do so with great pleasure. Paula Patterson directs the acting troupe, *Reflections*, at Shands, and my weekly participation with her group since 2000 made my third chapter possible. Helen King invited me to her ancient medicine conference at Reading, where I was able for the first time to present my ideas in a context beyond the classical world and the reception I received there further inspired this book; her request to publish my presentation as a chapter in her *Health in Antiquity* offered me welcome validation for my ideas. William Hall, whose workshops at Bay Area Theatre Sports I attended twice, helped me understand further the power of acting and taught me much of value. Susan Massad told me of the Performing the World Conferences, at which I learned about the role of drama in a wide range of contexts. Susanna Braund is responsible for the idea of bringing this book to this series; she saw my other work and asked if I was continuing in my pursuit of bringing the ancient and modern worlds together. I am deeply indebted to her question and giving my response a favourable reply.

Finally, but first in importance, I acknowledge the support and encouragement of my husband Kevin McCarthy. As author of more than three dozen books, he did not expect me to write in competition of his numbers, but he did remind me it was time to return to the computer and get on with my book; for that I am grateful. There were times when it was more fun to act than to write, so his prompting has been important in bringing my text to completion.

Glossary

Here I supply definitions for the Greek words used frequently in the text. These are words that appear on plans of the sanctuaries (*abaton*, *propylon*) or in the literature about the ancient Asklepieia (*iamata*, *anathêmata*) and so I have preferred to retain them.

abaton: dormitory, the hall in which the patients slept awaiting their dream visions.

anathêmata: dedicatory offerings hung in thanks at the sanctuary; they replicate the part of the body the deity has healed.

bothros: pit, for burning at some sites; at Asklepieia, for keeping the sacred snakes.

caduceus: the staff or wand of Hermes, messenger of the gods. In his hands two snakes surmount the simple staff.

estiatorion: dining hall; the word remains in modern Greek for 'restaurant'.

iamata: inscribed stelae which recorded the patients' dreams; those found at Epidauros give us the basic information about the 'dream therapy' practised at Asklepieia.

iatros: doctor; the word forms the root of many modern words in the medical profession, e.g. paediatrician, podiatrist.

katagôgion: hotel.

kathairesis: cleaning, here for the clearing up of offerings, a ritual performed regularly by the sanctuary attendants.

klepsydra: water-clock.

odeion: a small theatre (pl. ***odeia***), usually covered, whereas a normal theatre is in the open air.

paianistai: those who sang paeans, hymns of praise for the god.

peribolos: the surrounding wall of a sanctuary.

propylon: entry gate of a sanctuary; ***propylaia*** (pl.) refers to a multi-doored entrance.

stele: an upright stone slab with an inscribed or sculptured surface, usually on one side only (pl. **stelae**).

stoa: a hall colonnaded along one side, the basic structure of Greek public places.

tamata: the modern word for *anathêmata*, the thank-offerings dedicated at a shrine.

temenos: the boundary marking off a sacred site.

Introduction

In the dimly lit room a patient haltingly tells her story, how her sudden illness was affecting her, her concerns about her husband and children left at home. The actors listen respectfully, hearing the fear behind the patient's words. When she ceases speaking, the acting troupe quietly takes up a position by the bed. Using techniques learned through their training in Playback Theatre, they retell the patient's story as a mini-drama. Tears come to her eyes: someone understands how she really feels. At the close of the scene, the patient expresses her gratitude for the gift that the acting troupe has given her. She has been honoured, respected and reassured. Some weeks later, healed and on her way home, the patient told her doctors that while their skill had cured her disease, the visit by the drama troupe from the Arts-in-Medicine program had contributed greatly to her recovery from her illness.

Medicine and healing do not depend only on drugs and a physician's skill, for there is more to a patient than the physical problems which those treat. In order that an illness may be brought to a successful conclusion a patient's emotional and spiritual side must also be considered. It is often through an Arts-in-Medicine program that this aspect of a patient can be given care.

*

The flames leaped as oil was poured on the sacrificial cakes. Then the lights were put out and the patients lay down in the darkened *abaton*, each quietly praying to Asklepios to send a healing dream. As the sick and ailing drifted off to sleep, the god's priests and attendants came to the bedsides, laying their hands on the patients and administering healing ointments or whispering healing words. The actions of the bedside visitors echoed those of the actors playing the roles of Asklepios and his daughters which the patients had watched in the adjoining theatre just before retiring. In the morning, the patients

1

awoke and excitedly reported their dreams: they had seen the god standing beside their bed and had felt his hands upon them. The patients were cheered and, apparently, healed, or had instructions to guide them to health. Drama and dream had brought about a cure.

*

In his *Ploutos* Aristophanes reports actions very much like those described above: the flames, the darkened room, the visiting priests and attendants. While the comic playwright mixes humour into his report of what went on at the Asklepieion, his text must be based on actual experiences familiar to his audience. For his account suggests that the temple priests enacted the role of Asklepios; Karion reports that Asklepios himself appeared, accompanied by his daughters Panacea and Iaso. It is easy to posit that the priests had played the same roles earlier in the sanctuary's theatre, thus preparing the patients for the therapy offered while they slept and dreamed.

As we look back from current ideas on the interaction between drama and healing, on how both mental and emotional stimulation can help to restore health, can we discover the roots of these ideas in ancient Greece? Ancient texts frequently note that the conception of the god Asklepios himself was very similar to that of a doctor. Hippokrates (*Epidemics* I.xi) wrote that the art of medicine (a *technê*) had three parts: 'The disease, the patient, and the physician.' As the doctor is the servant of the art, 'the patient must cooperate with the physician in combating the disease'. These views are reflected in much current medical literature, that the physician and the patient work together in fighting the disease or illness. In his study of doctors, patients and placebos, Howard Spiro (1986: 35) writes:

> In ideal circumstances the intent of the physician, the frame of mind in which he gives the placebo, might even be seen as a joining with the patient in a confession of ignorance that we do not always know how the healing comes about, but we do know the force of the good patient-physician relationship.

Each year more and more doctors write books describing the crisis in modern medicine: that while the technical aspects of the contemporary tools for fighting disease are excellent, somehow the patient experiencing an illness has been forgotten. These doctors assert the need to return to the old ways, when there was a personal relationship between doctor and patient; in their discussions they frequently describe what they imagined once took place at the ancient sanctuaries of Asklepios.

Can this examination of our modern concepts of the relationship between health and art, especially drama, help us better understand what went on at the many sanctuaries of Asklepios? New work in psychoneuroimmunology indicates that the interaction between the psyche and the body plays a role in fighting disease; can this idea in some way be linked to what happened when a patient went to an Asklepieion? Finally, can the visit to a healing site such as Lourdes, or the very entry into a hospital, both of which are underscored by belief in the curing powers available there, be traced back to the ancient god of healing? And can that interaction also be tied to what the patient saw performed in the theatres of the Asklepieia? For archaeology has shown that theatres, or at least *odeia*, stand in or adjacent to the majority of the Greek sanctuaries dedicated to the god of healing.

In the following pages I first consider the interaction of body and psyche and its importance in conquering disease. Then I present some ideas about the nature of drama and the role it plays in healing, from the catharsis suggested by Aristotle to the rituals enacted against disease in primitive societies even today. I begin my examination of the ancient healing sanctuaries with a discussion of Asklepios and the legends associated with him. There follows a presentation on the process followed by patients who went to the healing sanctuary. I then address the evidence from archaeology, art, and text to show that drama played a part in the dream therapy practised in the ancient sanctuaries of the god.

In the second part of the book I offer a guided tour of the major Asklepieia of the Greek world. In this section my text describes the buildings at Epidauros and the other major sanctuaries, including Corinth, Messene, Oropos and Pergamon; after these I present a similar tour of such local sites as Dion, Lebena and Orchomenos. Here I also discuss the sanctuary to Asklepios at Athens, focusing upon where it was situated and why.

3

Introduction

From the site visits I return to the modern world and tell the story of drama as part of the Arts-in-Medicine program at Shands Hospital at the University of Florida. This story is based on my experience as an actress in the hospital drama troupe. In the final section of the book I discuss the conflict between Asklepios and Jesus in the early days of the Christian era. Then I show how ideas from the ancient cult of Asklepios continue into the modern world. These go beyond the hospital, where the Hippokratic oath and its prayer to the ancient deity hang in every doctor's office. Today we find the belief in a healing deity reborn in the churches dedicated to the healing saints, saints who have taken up residence where Asklepios used to dwell.

I

Drama and Healing in Contemporary Medicine

1. The Relationship Between Mind and Body

The wisdom of modern science is working to catch up with the wisdom of the ancient Greeks.

Jerome Groopman, *The Anatomy of Hope*, 207

Within the past several decades, the idea that medicine and art, especially dramatic art, can work together in the healing process has attracted the interest of those in the medical profession. While a story and movie such as *Patch Adams*[1] called wide public attention to the concept, for many years doctors have realized the therapeutic value of the arts for patients of all ages and with all types of illness. According to Dr John Graham-Pole, who established the Arts-in-Medicine program at Shands, art is therapeutic both for the creator and for the observer. It helps to displace negative feelings, enabling a person to view the existing situation more clearly and effectively. In his introduction to Graham-Pole's book (2000), Patch Adams writes, 'Creativity is a great medicine for all, both the creator and the one who experiences it. It is not an indulgence, it is fundamental to medical practice.' Adams, Graham-Pole and many of the doctors whose work is cited in this book understood that the bond between art and medicine was not a recent idea, that its roots lay with the ancient Greeks.[2]

Aristotle's well-known statement (*Poetics* 1449b27-8) that drama produces an emotional catharsis is often considered to have a continued validity and plays a role in the contemporary belief in the healing power of drama and the other arts. Aristotle's statement, however, described the response of a typical and healthy theatre audience, but its message, that drama can affect healing, is equally applicable to those who need to be healed.

Recent studies in medicine underscore and expand Aristotle's dic-

5

tum; they also work from Hippokrates' statement that physicians are in error when they separate the mind and soul from the body. In his treatise *On the Sacred Disease*, Hippokrates states clearly that even this affliction arises from natural causes. He writes (XVII.1), 'Men ought to know that from the brain, and from the brain only, arise our pleasures, joys, laughter, and jests, as well as our sorrows, pains, griefs and tears.' In short, as Simon (1978: 222) puts it, 'The first task of the doctor is to move the disease from the realm of mythology to the realm of physiology'; he continues by pointing out that nowhere in the Hippokratic writings, nor in the works of Galen, are mythological characters as portrayed on the Athenian stage used to illustrate any example of mental (or physical) illness.

On the subject of the unity of soul and body, and thus the relationship of doctor and patient, Hippokrates was equally clear that the two can not be separated. As Lloyd writes (1978: 60), 'While most of the anatomical, physiological, and pathological doctrines in the Hippocratic writings have long since been superseded, the ideal of the selfless, dedicated, and compassionate doctor they present has lost none of its relevance in the twentieth century.' Plato, too, urged an honest and caring relationship between doctor and patient. In *Laws* IV.720, he writes:

> The [physician] treats his patients' disease ... from the beginning in a scientific way, and takes the patient and his family into his confidence ... He does not give his prescriptions until he has won the patient's support, and when he has done so, he steadily aims at producing complete restoration to health by persuading the sufferer into compliance.

The beliefs of these ancient writers, Hippokrates, Aristotle and Plato, have recently found new followers, as those in medicine and medical research break away from the mind-body split set out by René Descartes. The French philosopher proclaimed that matter behaves according to physical laws and spirit is immaterial, and for two centuries Descartian dualism permeated western medical thought and research. His ideas finally began to be challenged in the later years of the twentieth century.

As the evidence from the new and growing field of psychoneuroimmunology indicates, good mental and emotional health lead to better bodily health. Psychoneuroimmunology may be defined as 'the scientific field of study investigating the link between bi-directional communications among the nervous system, the endocrine (hormone) system, and the immune system and the implications of these linkages for physical health'.[3] Psychoneuroimmunology (PNI) studies the interaction among the psychological, neurological and immunological systems, between the brain and the immune system. Those involved in this research believe that psychological experiences such as stress and anxiety can influence immune function, which in turn may have an effect on the course of a disease. Robert Ader and Nicholas Cohen did seminal work on PNI in 1975;[4] other scientists have been contributing to their work in an ever-growing number of studies. Neuropharmacologist Candace Pert, for example, discovered that chemical links (neuropeptides) reside in the cell walls of both the brain and the immune system. Her work showed the close association between the brain and the immune system, that emotions and health are interdependent.[5]

This rather new science tries to elucidate how the immune and nervous systems work with the psyche to help fight disease. In the initial work, PNI research focused on the material side of these interactions, as these are easier to study. Now those involved in PNI research are looking at how psychosocial components may influence immunity and its effects on health. While the importance of the psychological system in PNI is still difficult to define, clinical observations have shown how a positive mental condition, the body-mind relationship, assists the healing process.[6] Those who study PNI believe that they are providing modern scientific evidence for what went on at the ancient Asklepieia. As two psychopharmacologists put it (Song and Leonard, 2000: vi), 'Thus psychoneuroimmunoendocrinology has become the discipline that after 2500 years has served to unify the Hygeian and Asclepian schools of thought.'[7]

Placebo studies have also received serious medical attention in recent years. In these, an artificial world is created for the purpose of healing. Although giving a placebo is not done as an actual dramatic performance, the doctor administering it is involved in a pretended action. He acts, however, in a real situation. Howard Brody, who has devoted his career to the study of placebos and the response to them

7

writes (2000: 9) that the placebo response may be defined as 'A change in the body (or the body-mind unit) that occurs as the result of the symbolic significance which one attributes to an event or object in the healing environment.' He defines 'placebo' itself thus (14):

> In therapeutic healing, a placebo is a treatment modality or process administered with the belief that it possesses the ability to affect the body only by virtue of its symbolic significance. It can also be argued that the physician himself is an active agent in the so-called 'placebo effect'.

The relationship between a doctor and the patient is a dynamic that comes into the healing process. The patient believes the doctor can and will help his pain, and thus the attitude with which the doctor gives a placebo is important. Of the many who discuss the importance of the physician-patient relationship, Howard Spiro (1986) is perhaps most passionate. He asserts throughout his book that this is the key to the 'success' of the placebo. Spiro insists that never should science be laid aside, but that the impersonality of science must be tempered with the personal care and concern of the physician; that (242) 'the placebo is powerless without the physician'. He also notes that doctors who recognize the important link between their words and their actions believe they are following the advice of Hippokrates. The most important example passed on from 'the father of medicine' is the concern the physician must have for his patients. Numerous recent studies confirm his assertions.

In a recent placebo study it was discovered that even 'fake' surgical procedures could cure an ailment when the patient believed he had undergone actual surgery. Whether given pill or process, the patient got better. The author of the study describes the reason for the placebo cures:[8]

> What all explanations have in common … is the element of expectation, the promise of help on the way that can only be imparted by another human being. Hope can help soften the experience of illness, though it cannot cure the underlying disease … A compassionate and optimistic physician can be a walking placebo.

Role-playing was used in this study as well: an anesthetist visited one group of patients the night before their operation in a brusque quick manner, another group with a gentle sympathetic lengthy discussion. The second group 'required only half the amount of pain killing medication and were discharged an average 2.6 days earlier'.[9] The best, i.e. most objective, studies of the placebo effect now argue that the doctor who gives out the inert pill is not writing off the patient's complaint. Rather he understands that his attitude toward a patient's pain joins with the patient's need to believe that it can be cured; this combination leads to the remarkable number of successful placebo 'cures'.[10]

More evidence on the power of belief over reality appeared in the summer of 2002, when a placebo study reached the national headlines.[11] In this carefully monitored experiment, a type rarely carried out, it was shown that arthroscopic procedures for arthritis on the knee had no better result than placebo 'treatments'. Patients were sedated and when they awoke were told they had undergone arthroscopic surgery, but they actually were given sham (i.e. no) surgery. During the next two years, those who had the fake surgery actually surpassed in ability those who had received a real operation; they could climb stairs more easily and walk somewhat faster. Dr Bruce Moseley of Baylor College of Medicine in Houston who did the experiment states, 'What our study shows is that all of the benefit that people receive is from a placebo effect.' A TV interview with a patient confirmed he was pain-free and more mobile than he had been before the sham surgery. If these results can be attained in an atmosphere which promotes high-tech solutions to medical problems, how can it be doubted that the ritual/drama and dream therapy practised at Asklepieia brought 'medical' relief on a regular basis?

The placebo effect works with procedures that are not high tech as well, according to a study published in *Archives of Internal Medicine* and reported on ABC national news in September 2007.[12] Here Dr Heinz Endres of Ruhr-University and the others who directed the project found that patients with chronic back pain got substantial relief from acupuncture (which is not unexpected) but also from 'fake' acupuncture as well. Patients who had random needles inserted claimed to have relief; 48% of those interviewed said their pain decreased and they had to take less pain medication. Other doctors, such as Dr Scott Boden (Emory School of Medicine) and Dr Woodson Merrell (Beth Israel Medical Center), noted that, although they were surprised that sham acupuncture worked, it suggested that perhaps the very needle insertion provided 'a stimulus to an area of the body that tells the nervous system and brain to react. True acupuncture does the same thing, just with more consistent results.' Others suggested that the placebo effect was in play for these patients as well. All doctors who participated in or discussed the study, as well as those interviewed on ABC news, agreed that whether it was the acupuncture or the belief in the procedure, i.e. the placebo effect, the outcome was what was important.

The patient's need to believe has been underscored by the work of Yale oncologist Bernie Siegel. After seeing numerous cancer patients, he realized that many, if not most, of these wanted care more than cure. He changed his approach to those who came to him, realizing that they were people, not diseases. He became, in his own words, a healer, and his approach, in the words of his wife, became more 'clergical' than surgical.[13]

The writings of Brody, Siegel and others are further underscored by Katz (1984: 189-95), who focuses on the 'Placebo Effect of the Physician'. He addresses the issue of the disconnect between the effectiveness of the placebos which rests on the certainty with which the doctors prescribe them, and the uncertainty which the doctor must have in mind when he offers the pill. Katz argues that it is not the pill or potion that cures, but the attitude of the physician: patients believe that their doctor will provide a cure and that faith renders the prescribed placebo effective. While Katz is arguing the need for the modern doctor to admit the uncertainties which exist in modern medicine despite the numerous technical aids available to him, his discussion also addresses the issue of a patient's faith in his healer. He writes (192):

> If physicians themselves are the placebos, then they are powerful therapeutic agents in their own right. Their effectiveness is probably augmented by the positive transferences patients bring to their interactions with physicians ... Deep in patients' unconscious, physicians are viewed as miracle workers ... Medicine, after all, was born in magic and religion, and the doctor-priest-

magician-parent unity that persists in patients' unconscious cannot be broken.

These words (again) confirm that the patients who came to an Asklepieion brought with them their expectation of a cure. As Galen pointed out, patients preferred to believe the advice of the god over that of the physician, even when it seemed counter to good sense. He writes in his commentary on Hippokrates (Edelstein T-401), 'It has great influence on the patient's doing all which is prescribed if he has been firmly persuaded that a remarkable benefit to himself will ensue.'

A significant number of studies shows a link between active religious belief and good health. Epidemiological research cites numerous examples of the healing power of prayer, that science confirms the positive effects of *theosomatic* medicine.[14] Contemporary research in many areas, then, confirms that we can believe that the ancient god of healing did, in fact, heal.

> Prometheus: I caused mortals to cease foreseeing doom.
> Chorus: What cure did you provide them with against that sickness?
> Prometheus: I placed in them blind hopes.
> Chorus: That was a great gift you gave to men.
>
> Aeschylus, *Prometheus Bound*, 250-3

Hope, the gift which the Titan gave to mankind, remains a great boon. In the normal course of events, Prometheus' gift makes us get up in the morning; each day we expect to live, prosper and enjoy life. Hope may be blind – it is based on nothing tangible, but it keeps mortals willing and able to face their daily lives. It also plays a role in health and healing. Those who believe that hope can assist a patient in attaining a more positive mental outlook add a further component to the answers sought by those involved in PNI research. One of the most compelling accounts of the power of hope is the first person narrative of oncologist-hematologist Jerome Groopman. In *The Anatomy of Hope* (2004) Groopman presents case studies of several of his patients who faced their illness with hope and how that helped them come to a good outcome or, in some cases, a good death.

In his last chapters, Groopman writes in the first person. He

11

himself suffered bungled back surgery and lived a decade in dire pain. Finally he found Dr Jim Rainville, who told him he could overcome this pain with the right attitude. As Groopman recovered, he became fascinated with the processes of 'alternative' medicine that he had originally scorned. As he learned more about PNI work and placebo studies, he came to realize that the mental approach of the patient was, indeed, important, and he had the best possible witness to its success, himself. He came to believe that there was a biology of hope; his research showed that belief and expectation (i.e. hope) 'can block pain by releasing the brain's endorphins and enkephalins, thereby mimicking the effects of morphine' (170). Groopman continues, citing works of others who study placebos, and concludes that the attitude of the physician as the authority figure plays the role of the shaman of ancient rituals.

Today a doctor can offer patients the latest and best in medical technology; those who seek help from their doctors believe they will receive the medicines and procedures to cure them. Those who went to the sanctuaries of Asklepios believed the same: the god would give them appropriate treatments to restore their health. Both groups bring their belief, their faith, their hope with them. Groopman (2004: 207) sums up his studies of the role of hope in modern medicine in a single sentence that ties the two worlds together: 'The wisdom of modern science is working to catch up with the wisdom of the ancient Greeks.'

Nor does the modern physician banish the ancient divinity from his hospital. On every doctor's office hangs the text of the Hippokratic oath, a testament to the medical work and beliefs of the 'father of medicine.' Above or beside this text is imprinted the symbol of the medical profession: the rod entwined atop with twin serpents. That this was not, in fact, the emblem of Asklepios but is rather the *caduceus* or wand of Hermes, matters not, for rod and serpent, other-wise entwined, *were* the attributes of the healing god.[15] Amid the high-tech machines and training of today's physician, the influence of the two healing forces from ancient Greece, doctor and divinity, is remembered.

Many a modern doctor looks for assistance to other realms besides science. While medicine and sophisticated technological treatment are never scorned, the role of art, as expressed in painting, poetry, and drama, is ever more recognized in the healing process: the power of science and that of the humanities can work together in providing a patient with the best possible care.

2. Art and Medicine

> Tragedy is a collective dream or rite, not merely in terms of narrative content, but also in dramatic process — how it is staged, how it appears to us. [One comes] to Epidauros not just to see a play but to partake of the ancient ritual of healing.
>
> Edward Tick, *The Practice of Dream Healings*, 11-12

The idea that drama and healing are related can be traced to ancient times. I noted previously the belief that Aristotle's familiar dictum (*Poetics* 1449b27-8) that tragedy effects 'a catharsis through pity and terror' has relevance to contemporary theatre as therapy. However, while the idea of a catharsis brought about by watching drama might seem to be desirable, the 'pity and terror' aroused by the Greek tragedies better applies to a healthy audience whom the playwrights expected to acquire wisdom through the suffering vicariously shared with the mythic characters on stage. Thus it cannot be that the plays performed in the ancient Asklepieia were those seen at the theatre of Dionysos. Nevertheless, a link between drama and healing can be shown, and its roots do lie in ancient Greek belief and ritual. As Simon (1978: 143-4) argues, one can consider theatre as therapy in a different framework than the 'catharsis' of Aristotle's text – although Simon points out that there are many different ways to view those words and we cannot be sure exactly what Aristotle meant by them. Simon, who is a psychiatrist with classical training, sees 'similarities between what one derives from drama and what one derives from psychoanalytic insight ... Good therapy and good theatre have in common a set of inner processes.'

Simon further asserts that drama offers the audience an enlarged view of the possibilities of life as they watch the struggles of the heroic figures on stage. He writes (145), 'Insofar as good drama can enable an individual to undergo some of the inner rearrangements here described [an enlarged view of the possibilities open in relationships to the self and to others], theatre can initiate or advance a therapeutic

13

process.' I noted in the previous section Graham-Pole's discussion of how the creative arts and healing work together, and it is these ideas that I want to develop further here.

Drama, the enactment of a life story, encourages the mind to become involved in the situations portrayed in the story; it permits a viewer to consider and vicariously experience the events portrayed. The acts on stage replay the acts of life. As the audience watches and listens, they respond, Simon says (1978: 83), as do those listening to a bard; they are involved with their eyes and ears and 'with the mind and entire nervous system.' The interrelationship between mind and emotion, as confirmed by PNI studies, is at work in the theatre audience.

The stage is, in many ways, a sacred space. It is set apart from the ordinary, marked off by definite boundaries as a sanctuary was defined by the bordering *temenos* in the ancient world. Thus, as Pendzik (1994: 31) writes, 'The close link between the stage and the sacred space leads us to assume that, as an extension of the latter, the stage too is a therapeutic place.'

In many traditional cultures, wounds, illness, or psychological disturbances are addressed by dramatic rituals performed by shamans or community healers.

Anthropological research shows again and again how the medicine man (or woman), the shaman, leads a patient to health. These figures, respected by their communities, often try to drive out the cause of the illness by both ritual actions and, more importantly, ritual words. Since patients, family members, and the shaman believe the body's distress comes either from a spell cast by a force of evil or by the invasion of such a figure, i.e. a witch or demon, it makes sense to use word and action to attack the evil spirit. When the patient comes to the shaman, a place for the contest is marked off as a sacred space of healing, and certain preliminary rites are performed by all those gathered there: patient, shaman, and members of the community, for healing is generally considered to be a community experience. The danger of the illness, now afflicting a single individual, might easily spread to others, so a cleansing of the community is believed to be necessary.

The shaman begins the healing rituals. The aim of these rituals is, most often, healing; the goal is not necessarily to cure.[16] It is important to note the distinction between the two, and it is a distinction which

14

carries to the developed world where the physician strives to cure the disease but often forgets to address the illness. In recent years, many writers, both doctors and their patients, again and again address this failure of modern medicine. Most of the authors included in my bibliography discuss it passionately; they see the inability of the doctor to recognize the disconnect between disease and illness as a major stumbling block for those who practise the medical profession and those who seek its aid.

In traditional societies, then, healers were recognized by the community for their special powers to use dramatic word and action in their attempt to conquer illness. In the Greek world, the sanctuary personnel enacted rituals portraying Asklepios and his attending daughters healing their patients. Artwork illustrating these scenes shows that the sacred serpent and dog were also in the god's retinue. These performances prepared the patients for their sleep in the *abaton*; it also served to unite them with each other and with the god. As Renée Emunah (1994: 21) writes:

> Healing rituals have the capacity to express and embody the emotional, the mental and the spiritual, the personal and the universal, the secular and the sacred. The person, group or community to be healed is viewed holistically... Drama is the art form that most clearly encompasses the [other arts] and from which the others stem.

Thus when the patients at the ancient Asklepieia saw the ritual dramas before retiring to sleep, they were prepared for the god's ministrations both by the emotions the actors aroused and by their belief in Asklepios' ability to cure.

A further link between what is enacted on the stage and the healing dreams the patient experienced may rest upon another way in which the immune system responds to mental stimulation. Recent studies show that *guided imagery* can assist people to control consciously their immune responses. Guided imagery encourages patients to focus upon their immune response systems, e.g. upon the white cells which must attack a disease. As reported in Hafen *et al.* (1996: 35-7) those who did so were able, in many cases, to reduce the spread of cancer and even the size of tumors. Patients at the ancient Asklepieia who watched a pageant showing the god healing could then apply that image to their own situation: they could imagine the god healing them. This would also explain the nature of their dreams: 'I saw the god beside me and he did this *to me.*'[17]

The carved stone stelae which depict Asklepios healing are executed in a style similar to those which illustrate dramatic performances or stories based on familiar myths. The consistency in style of all such narrative stelae suggests that these were mass-produced to be displayed at the sanctuaries in the same way as were the standardized *anathêmata* available (apparently) for purchase on site. Nevertheless there is sufficient variation in the stelae stories to suggest that the dedicant directed the artist, or at least chose for the god a stele that best represented his/her dream.

Sandtray therapy is another method of art therapy used to encourage patients, especially cancer patients, to give expression to their experience of the disease. As cancer is an illness which threatens not only the whole body but also the emotional, social and spiritual aspects of a person's life, patients often need more than a paintbrush or craft set to express what is happening to them. Sandtray therapy has been shown to be particularly effective in assisting patients to present their fears, their hopes and their dreams. Lusebrink (1999: 87-9) writes that the function of dreams is to bring together previous knowledge and current experience, that a dream states a problem and possible solutions for the emotions it arouses. She continues, 'The dreamer's emotional state upon awakening in the morning is influenced by the dream mood ... [and] dreams in illness can provide important sources of information about the nature and location of the illness.' Her words recall those of Hippokrates, who wrote that a patient's dreams often gave clues as to his illness; indeed, in *Regimen* IV Hippokrates offers an entire listing of what kind of sickness each dream indicates.[18]

Sandtray therapy provides patients with a tray of sand and a collection of figurines and objects with which to give spatial and figurative expression to their dreams. It helps patients gain control over their illness by setting up a series of scenes in the sand; by the very act of creating these sand tray scenes the patients can work out issues of fear, anger, acceptance and hope. This particular form of art therapy gives a three-dimensional picture; it looks to both viewer and creator like a drama on stage. Even when the patients do not use the figurines to enact the scenes they have created – it can remain a static art form – the succession of constructed scenes allows the patients to develop a fuller expression of their emotions and their pain. Lusebrink describes the process and the purpose thus (91):

> Sandtray therapy lends itself to dream representations through displaying the most important dream scenes in the same tray and portraying dream actions with the figurines. Dreams represent a continuation of the dreamer's waking life experiences and reenact her intrapersonal concerns.

However, when the patients choose to use role-playing with the figures, the therapy opens up further ways to explore their concerns. Lusebrink (93) suggests that 'for cancer patients these ways of interacting are important, because their active participation in the treatment and decision making may help the individual to regain some sense of control.' The acting *out* of these emotions underscores the premise put forth by Graham-Pole (2000: 138), 'Seeing this little piece of your life from the perspective of a play helps you step outside the real-life drama and even have a little more control over the way your life's unfolding.'

Although Shakespeare's 'All the world's a stage' is often quoted[19] and most people would agree that all aspects of life are enacted on its space, in the contemporary world drama has been, for the most part, left to (if not relegated to) the theatre proper; plays are written to be performed in a commercial or community theatre. When drama is performed in a hospital, as it is at Shands Hospital at the University of Florida, it becomes a uniquely vital form that plays a role in the patients' healing process. Again, as Emunah (1994: xv-vi) has written, 'Drama, by its very nature, induces empathy and perspective ... Sometimes it is only through conceiving the future and remembering the past that we can bear the present.' Because drama unites past and future in the present, it offers a way to bear the present, and for those who must endure illness in that present drama helps them take the first step to a successful healing.

II

Drama and Healing in Ancient Greece

1. The Cult of Asklepios

The God

'I come from holy Trikka, a god whom his mother bore in wedlock
with Apollo, Asklepios, skilful king of medical wisdom.'

> Asklepios describing himself, from
> Eusebius, *Praeparatio Evangelica*
> III.14.6 (Edelstein T-13)

The Greek god of healing, Asklepios, was said to be the son of Apollo
by a mortal woman. He was a man conceived from a god, a mortal who
became an excellent physician, a man whose skill earned him heroic
status. Herakles earned his place as a hero through his physical skill,
Theseus through his political acumen, Asklepios by his medical knowledge. He, as other Greek heroes, would pass through the Realm of the
Dead and be resurrected to life on earth. There he would remain a
terrestrial divinity and would not ascend to Mt Olympus: Asklepios
was needed on earth to heal mortal men and women.

In most accounts, the woman who bore Asklepios was Koronis,
daughter of the Thessalian prince Phlegyas. While some accounts say
the god's mortal mother was Arsinoe, daughter of the Messenian
Leucippus, Koronis is usually named his mother. His generation is
celebrated in the opening lines of the seventh-century BC *Homeric
Hymn to Asklepios:*

I begin to sing of Asklepios, healer of diseases
and son of Apollo. Noble Koronis, daughter of
King Phlegyas, bore him on the plain of Dotion
to be a great joy for men and charm evil pains away.
And so hail to you, O lord! I pray to you in my song.

18

The traditional tale does not make Koronis so noble: she did not remain faithful to her immortal (and thus absent) lover, but took up with a local peasant, Ischys, who would grow old as she would. Pindar (*Pythian* III) declares that Koronis was shot dead by an arrow of Artemis by the design of Apollo because 'she accepted a second marriage ... [although] carrying the immaculate seed of the god;' thus, Pindar continues, she was a mortal who hunted 'impossibilities on the wings of ineffectual hopes'. Told of her infidelity by a raven (or a crow), Apollo in quick anger killed her, or asked his sister Artemis to do the deed. In his rage he also turned the reporting bird, then white, to black. But then, overcome by grief for his hasty action, he snatched the unborn child from the burning funeral pyre. It was an unusual birth, medically speaking, and perhaps Apollo's skill in this method of delivery set the child on his way to medical learning (Wells 1998: 14).[1] Apollo entrusted the baby to the wise centaur Cheiron to raise. In many accounts, it was Cheiron who instructed Asklepios in the arts of healing.[2]

The place of the divinity's birth and first cult, however, varies in location depending upon the storyteller. The oldest account places his early life and first healing site in northern Greece, in Trikka (modern Trikkala), although there is little textual or archaeological evidence for this version. In the *Iliad* (II.729-33) Homer describes how the sons of Asklepios, Machaon and Podaleirios, led troops from that area and were revered for their knowledge of healing those wounded in battle. It is they who take centre stage in the stories of medical skill; Asklepios remains behind, both in story and importance.

While this is the Thessalian version, that told at Epidauros is rather different and is the one which becomes the standard story. In the Epidaurian account, Koronis gave birth to the child (still that of Apollo) when visiting the area with her father. In her shame she abandoned the infant on the slopes of Mt Myrtium. But divine off-spring cannot die. Thus goats nursed the child and the herd dog guarded him. This child's story unfolded rather differently from that of Romulus and Remus, found and raised by the shepherd Faustulus. For when a local herdsman discovered the baby Asklepios, he was frightened away when lightning flashed about the child's head. Recognizing this as a divine warning that the child was under the protection of a god, he left the infant to be raised by the goats and dog. These two beasts left their mark on the later cult: no goat was ever sacrificed to Asklepios, and the dog became his faithful companion, sharing with the god and the serpent the ability to heal. In time, according to the more traditional version, the youth came to his father's sanctuary in Epidauros, where the Olympian deity was known as Apollo Maleatis and joined him in curing illness via dreams.

Apollo was the divinity in charge both of disease and of death from disease and of healing from illness or wound. As Homer shows in his *Iliad* (e.g. I.33-100), the god responds to prayers to bring both, restoring health to one who honours him appropriately, sending a plague upon those who fail to do so. While the divinity could and would heal anywhere, special sites developed around the Greek world for those seeking a cure from Apollo. Epidauros was a well-known sanctuary to Apollo, but the god also cured at other places. He had a healing sanctuary at Pergamon, as the *Iliad* indicates (V.445-8); Apollo apparently pre-dated Asklepios at Corinth, and at Kos Asklepios joined his father as healer in an already established cult centre; Pausanias (e.g. III.22.9 and VIII.225.10) notes several lesser sites with similar stories. But Apollo, like the other Olympians, could be an arbitrary god who both offered cure and sent disease. There was a need for a healing divinity, and to fulfil that need, the cult of Asklepios came into being.

Born of mortal woman, Asklepios was not immediately divine, but first a culture hero, a man whose engendering was by a deity and who had a special skill. In the early accounts, Asklepios heals by such means as other physicians; he is just better at it and is honoured for his healing art. The ambiguity of Asklepios' origins rests partially upon the fact that he was a hero before he was a god, and thus the story of his origin is more appropriate to a mortal than a divinity. Asklepios' biography then is brief; little is known about his life, as a man or a hero. In sum, he was engendered by a god, born of mortal woman, married, had children, and died: he was a *heros*. He is recognized as a physician with power.[3] Thus in the Homeric text Asklepios was the father of the healer-warriors, Machaon and Podaleirios, while he himself played no role at Troy. In all accounts, Epione is his wife and mother of the sons who learned healing and the daughters who represent its aspects. In the epic world, his importance rests upon the medical skill he imparted to these sons; at Troy, Machaon's defining epithet is 'son of the blameless physician Asklepios'. As the Edelsteins put it (II.9), 'Machaon and Podalirius are physicians rather than warriors, craftsmen rather than kings'. But the warriors at Troy respected them for their healing ability and called upon them when wounded, as did Agamemnon when struck by an arrow (*Iliad* IV.212-19). There were others among the Greek warriors who possessed some medical skill; for example, when Machaon himself is wounded, Patroklos takes up the care of the wounded Eurypylos (*Iliad* IX.821-47). The latter, indeed, employs all the actions Hippokrates will later recommend: he treats Eurypylos' wound and then stays by him to offer post-operative care until he is recalled to battle. Homer informs us that Patroklos had learned his medical ability from Achilles, who had learned it from Cheiron himself. Important to note is that the healing skills in which Cheiron trained his pupils are entirely based on drugs and surgery; there is no dream therapy in Homer's tales.

Unlike other deities of the Greek pantheon, Asklepios had but one sphere of influence. His primary interest lay in fighting disease. Unlike his father Apollo, he never sent disease or used it as a weapon against those who may have angered him. Although Apollodorus (*Bibliotheca*, Edelstein T-3) says that Athena gave him the dual-powered Gorgon blood, to be used 'for the bane of mankind', the deity apparently never availed himself of this deadly potion. In his consistent kindness to mortals, Asklepios differs not only from other Greek divinities but from other pagan gods as well. Kinsley (1996: 3) writes, '[In most traditional cultures] illness is associated with spiritual beings such as gods, goddesses [and other spirits] .... When humans offend them in some way, they are often provoked to send illness.'

In his zest for healing, however, Asklepios even sought to conquer death, and in doing so he finally went too far and restored a dead man to life.[4] Not only did this anger Zeus, who saw the son of Apollo violating the basic laws of fate, but also Hades complained to his brother about Asklepios' healing arts: so many were getting better that the Realm of the Dead was lacking souls. For his excess (either restoration or over-healing) Zeus hurled a thunderbolt at him, casting him into the realm of the dead.[5] Garland (1992: 117) remarks that the thunderbolt was perhaps 'a painful reminder of the necessary and inevitable limits of medical expertise'. Whatever the reminder, the violent act of Zeus aroused Apollo to battle his father. In his anger he killed the Cyclopes, who make the thunderbolts, and in response Zeus sent his angry son into a year's servitude to Admetus, King of Thessaly. There, too, Apollo continued to confuse the realms of living and dead by offering Admetus a way to escape his own death; Euripides tells the story in his *Alkestis*.

But Asklepios as culture hero could not be so easily forgotten. He soon earned veneration as a hero, then as a chthonic god, an underworld figure who can bring blessings to those who visit the site of his death. His legend asserts that at some point he was restored to life and elevated to a divine status. It is his time in the underworld and his subsequent restoration that earns Asklepios both his chthonic association and his pure divinity – his mortality was burned off by the blast of Zeus and his time in Hades' realm. But he is more than a mortal who became a *heros*. For although he is a hero, Asklepios has no grave, no single spot set off by ritual. He is, rather, worshipped throughout the Greek and Roman world in temples graced with marble or chryselephantine statues.

Because of his time in the underworld, the serpent becomes his associate and is at times identified with him. The snake was always thought to be a divine creature, one always closely related to any earth-cult, for it has the ability to live both above and below earth, it renews itself every spring by the shedding of its skin, it strikes quickly and it can kill but is also believed to heal. This mysterious creature, both attractive and fearful, plays a role in many religious rites. The serpent was associated with several of the ancient gods, such as Athena, Hekate and Demeter, as well as with eastern deities, nor was the theriomorphic appearance of the god limited to the cult of Asklepios. Garland (1992: 121) notes that 'theriomorphism represents a very ancient strand of Greek religion, one which was overlaid but never entirely supplanted by anthropomorphism'.

After his death Asklepios does not ascend to Mt Olympus. He remains on earth where his healing arts are needed. Asklepios, the prototype of the good doctor, the one who protects from death by disease and restores mortals to health, was frequently designated a *daimon,* a distinction which in his case marks him as a 'terrestrial god'. Asklepios did not ascend to the realm of the gods on Mt Olympus nor dwell below the earth: he was neither an Olympian nor a Chthonian. He was attended by his family, each a personification of an abstract iatric concept, e.g. Iaso (wound), Panacea (cure-all), and Hygieia (health). The latter was the most important of his daughters, the one who, according to Stafford (2005: 120-35), works most often with him and is represented most frequently in art. The ambiguity of Asklepios' 'life' is reflected in his offspring: his sons are always portrayed as mortals with good medical skill, while his daughters are considered to share their father's divinity. Hygieia, indeed, often has her own temple and shares in the cults of other true Olympian deities. Hypnos (Sleep) and Oneiros (Dream) were reportedly present also at some sanctuaries; perhaps those who recorded their presence considered them necessary attendants for the god who healed the sick through their dreams.

The god restored patients to health in many ways, some of which are clearly rather bizarre; others follow such techniques as would be consistent with those of the mortal *iatros*. Pindar (*Pythian* III.50-8) describes some of the ways the god cured: 'some he treated with gentle incantations, some he healed with potions to drink, others he bandaged with medications widely gathered and he set some on their feet again by surgery'. It is interesting to note that Pindar, like Homer, credits Asklepios with the techniques of doctors, making no mention of therapy via dreams.

Despite the fact that Asklepios never attained a place on Mt Olympus, he was never a regional deity with an identified tomb (as were, for instance, Amphiaraos and Trophonios). The god of healing, with his staff and serpent, walked among mortals, curing their sickness at an ever-growing number of sanctuaries around the ancient world. Unlike other gods, he was always accessible and never really punished those who offended him. If someone failed to believe in his powers – the one 'offence' anyone ever committed against him – he merely chided them, often by healing them so as to disprove their doubt. He was a god who laughed at the foibles of mortals and from time to time teased them. Once Ithmonice, a woman of Pellene, asked to be pregnant; when Asklepios questioned her as to any other wishes, she said she had none. After a three-year pregnancy she returned to him and made the second part of the request: that she bring forth a healthy child. The god laughed and as soon as she was outside the sanctuary she gave birth (*IG* IV² I Stele A.ii = Edelstein T-423.2). Another one of the *iamata* records a similar example of the god's good nature (*IG* IV² I

Stele A.viii = Edelstein T-423.8). When Euphanes, a local lad, came to the god to be cured of 'stone', he dreamed the god stood near him and asked what he would give should he be cured. 'Ten dice', the boy said. The god laughed and said he would cure him, and the next morning the boy walked out cured.

When patients came to a sanctuary of Asklepios, the statues they saw of the deity always portrayed him as a kindly god. He was the idealization of the physician: bearded and apparently of middle age, but always larger than life. He wore an ankle-length cloak fastened on the left shoulder and sandals; unlike the Olympian deities, he was never portrayed unclothed.[6] The god always had his walking staff, entwined with the sacred snake, and often his dog accompanied him. Whether standing or seated, Asklepios seemed to invite mortals to approach him, to trust in his skill. There were many images of the god in his sanctuaries: in the temple, of course, by the altar, probably by the *abaton*. The statues were usually of marble, but the cult image might be gold and ivory like that of Athena at the Parthenon; the statue at Epidauros was said to be chryselephantine. The patients would also see the dedicatory inscriptions, the stelae showing the deity in action, the *anathêmata* and any special gifts donated in gratitude for a special cure. The god's presence was evident throughout his sanctuary. He did not appear in sudden epiphanies which quieted all of nature, but the power of his presence was as evident to the patients as is the power of God or Christ in a church or healing centre today.

The walking staff entwined with serpent was the identifying attribute of Asklepios, as was the lyre with Apollo, the club with Herakles, the owl and the spear with Athena. Since Asklepios spent his days travelling the world and his nights walking the *abaton*, the staff is a natural attribute. In time it becomes a symbol for the healing arts and comes to indicate the god's special ability. Later writers would credit it with various powers; the knots, for example, were supposed to represent the difficulty of healing, or the entwined serpent was said to indicate the preservation of body and soul (Edelstein II.227-8).[7]

Whatever the rod-and-serpent may have meant to the ancients, it took on a life of its own in the post-classical world. Asklepios' use of it was just one of many reasons that he so challenged the early Christians, for they were more than a little uncomfortable with the fact that he shared with Jesus the ability to do miracles with rods and snakes.

But the real development of the staff came in the Renaissance, when it became a printers' mark for *pharmacopoeia.* Soon the rod-and-staff, separated from the ancient god, began to appear in paintings of prominent men of medicine. For example, in Jacob Houbraken's etched portrait of the English physiologist and embryologist William Harvey, who discovered the circulation of blood, the rod and serpent lie beneath the portrait medallion (Schouten, 1967: 128). In time Asklepios' staff would be adopted by various medical associations, and is the official symbol of the American Medical Association.

More interesting is the transformation of Asklepios' staff to the wand of Hermes, the *caduceus,* as the symbol for medicine. According to *Homeric Hymn* IV, Hermes acquired his staff from Apollo; in the *Hymn* Apollo identified it (528-30) as a wonderful staff of riches and wealth: 'It is made of gold with three branches and it will keep you safe from all harm.' Apollo meant, of course, it would protect Hermes as the herald of the gods, but the words were later misinterpreted. Thus the *caduceus* of Hermes, which was not a medical symbol in antiquity, has become such a symbol since the Renaissance. As a symbol of life and abundance, Hermes' *caduceus* shared properties with Asklepios' staff. The god heals the sick, snatching them from death; Hermes leads souls to (and away from) the grave. It soon replaced the rod and serpent as the frontispiece of seventeenth-/eighteenth-century phar-macopoeias.[8]

The popularity of Hermes' staff as a symbol for medicine probably arose from the ever-growing popularity of alchemy. As the alchemist sought to turn ordinary metal to gold, he found other chemical trans-formations, many of which led to the discovery of new pharmaceutical products (Schouten, 1967: 120-3). Furthermore, as Hermes Trismeg-istus, the Egyptian version of the god, became ever better known, it was almost inevitable that the two symbols would become confused. But it did not become an official symbol of the medical profession in America until the early 1900s. The story of its erroneous but quick development is worth noting.

The USA Medical Corps (USAMC) had designed a new uniform, and at the suggestion of an assistant surgeon, Captain Frederick Reynolds, the *caduceus* became a collar insignia for all personnel in the USAMC. He was, apparently, unaware of the distinction between the staff of Asklepios and that of Hermes. The Surgeon General to

25

whom Reynolds first suggested the symbol dismissed his idea; the next Surgeon General to assume the office, however, accepted it. On 17 July 1902, the gold *caduceus* was adopted as the insignia of the USA Medical Corps. Even though the error was later noticed, it was too late: soon the *caduceus* of Hermes became the popular symbol for medicine. However, the proper Asklepieian staff entwined with serpent as the insignia of the AMA is usually printed on the copy of the Hippokratic Oath which hangs on the office wall of every modern physician.

The son of Apollo survived beyond belief in his father or many of the other Olympians; indeed his power was revered for centuries. For Asklepios was a deity who more than any other touched the lives of mortals when he cured those who came to him. Sometimes the god acted in a most direct manner; at other times the remedies his patients reported were strange, the stuff of dreams or, perhaps, at the moment of his visitation, nightmares. But upon awaking, those who had sought his help realized they had received it.

The sanctuaries of Asklepios now lie in ruins and many of his images are lost. But his ideas live on in every doctor's office in that framed copy of the Oath of Hippokrates. In its words the god of healing and the first doctor's words are united, underscoring again that in antiquity the two did not stand in opposition. As Asklepios was said to be the son of a god and a mortal, in his actions he reflected both sides of his engendering: he showed the healing power of Apollo and the compassion of his humanity. Edward Tick (2001: 265) writing about the god who had transgressed his mortal limits and imagining that Asklepios was speaking to him, beautifully sums up the 'life' story of this hero who became a god:

> [He was telling me] that at that moment when he seemed to promise human beings the possibility of immortality, his grand-father, the ruler of heaven and protector of cosmic justice, slew him with a thunderbolt. That he was then brought up to live with the gods. And that now, he has all eternity to spend visiting those who suffer, bringing them healing or the means of healing through his dreams and visions.

Asklepios, the god of the Greek pantheon unique for his constant care and compassion for mortals, no longer has sanctuaries dedicated to

26

him, nor does he move to new sites in theriomorphic guise. He no longer receives a cock in sacrifice. But he has survived past his time in both his ancient symbols and in the recent recognition that the mind and the body work together toward health, a teaching Asklepios brought via dreams to those who believed in him.

The Process

> The night lamps flicker low, casting snaky patterns across the colonnade … All at once the fitful eyes of a man see between the candle-lamp and the wall the shadow of an upraised serpent, a great yellow snake with topaz eyes. It slides closer. It is arched and godlike. It bends above him, swaying, the tongue and the lamplight flickering as one. Exultant, he raises himself upon one arm and with the other, reaches out for the touch that heals.
>
> Richard Selzer, *Mortal Lessons: Notes on the Art of Surgery,* 33

Asklepios sent healing dreams. In the inner space of the *abaton*, it was not the doctor but the god who brought those dreams to fulfilment. At all sanctuaries of the god, the divinity came to those sleeping within its boundaries to bring a cure. He might appear in his own form, as a kindly man with a staff, or as a snake; from time to time the deity took on the characteristics of a dog. If the god appeared as a man, he would cure by touch or directive, advising the sleeping patient what he or she should do to be well. If Asklepios approached as a snake or dog, the animal would lick the patient's afflicted part, curing by the magic of its divine tongue. For the most part, the god only worked his miracles at his sanctuaries; patients had to go to an Asklepieion to be cured.[9]

The ancients believed in the validity of dreams. Literature from Homer through the dramatists portrays people prompted to action by what they saw in a dream; history reports real people doing the same. Homer writes of Agamemnon taking up the battle again (*Iliad* II.6-16 – albeit misguided deliberately by the gods) and Nausikaa gathering the laundry to be washed (*Odyssey* VI.15-40); it is worth noting that in Homer's texts the dream figure represents someone whom the dreamer knows. Characters in the tragedies tend to have dreams showing themselves in action: Klytemnestra determined to send offerings to the tomb of Agamemnon after she dreamed she gave birth to a snake (*Choephoroe* 32-41) and Iphigeneia decided to spare no more Greeks after she saw herself marking her brother for sacrifice (*Iphigeneia in Tauris* 42-55/ 348-50). Hekabe's dreams in her play are somewhat different. Her nightmare had two parts: she saw the death of her son Polydoros and the sacrifice of her daughter Polyxena (*Hekabe* 67-98). In this script we know these dreams are true, because the ghost of Polydoros had just spoken the prologue, telling us how he was murdered and that Achilles' ghost had demanded the blood of his sister. As Euripides' play unfolds, Hekabe discovers that her dreams were true. These are but several examples of dreams in drama; the choral imagery of the tragedies is also rich in dreams.

Real people also took action on the basis of dreams. Dodds (1951: 108) cites several examples of 'godsent' dreams, dreams which prescribe a dedication; he notes that there are 'numerous inscriptions stating that their author makes a dedication "in accordance with a dream" or "having seen a dream" '. The dream sent by the gods is properly termed the *theopemptos*; it comes to the dreamer as a result of prayers or sacrifices.

Nor was the belief that a dream could heal limited to those who visited an Asklepieion. In his *Sacred Diseases,* Aelius Aristides, the second-century AD orator, wrote extensively of his many ailments and how Asklepios directed him to seek their cure. Almost all of his actions seem to result from his very explicit dreams; he follows what the god orders, even when the prescribed actions seem contrary to good sense. Galen himself attributes his pursuit of a medical career to a dream had by his father. He later wrote an entire treatise on dreams, in which he describes how the nature of a patient's dream can help determine the imbalance of his humours. He sums up his discussion by asserting (*On Diagnosis in Dreams,* conclusion), 'What our patients see in their visions-in-sleep often indicates to us both the shortage or abundance and the quality of their humours.' Even before Galen, Hippokrates had credited the power of dreams. Noting that the mind is distracted during the day, he asserted that at night the soul performs all functions of the body. 'Therefore,' he writes (*Regimen* IV.86), 'he who knows how to interpret aright these acts [of the soul during sleep] knows a great part of wisdom.' While usually the god's directives are straightforward, at times the cures are hidden within puns. Oberhelman (1981: 420) argues that 'puns form an integral part of the majority of dreams and that the interpretations involve the explication of wordplay'. The words of Apollo's son, Asklepios, like those of his Pythia, often need interpretation. Once deciphered, however, the dreamer always begins to take the directed action.

When reporting their dreams, or when dreams were analyzed (as Hippokrates did those of his patients), the Greeks always said that they *saw* a dream; they never said they *had* a dream. In earlier times the general belief was that the gods sent a dream, a vision which took on the form of a familiar person who stood by the head of the dreamer. Although Hippokrates recognized that dreams arose from the human psyche, the terminology used to describe the night-time vision remained the same: a patient saw a dream; he did not have one. Thus the cultural context in which people came to an Asklepieion was such that it would be natural for them to say 'I saw Asklepios standing by me'; 'I saw his serpent lick my wound.'

The priests and attendants at the healing sanctuaries played a role in the process. It was they who taught the patients how to eat properly, exercise, bathe, and take up other practices that would lead to a more healthy life. The priests were busy, too, directing the sacrifices, collecting the offerings, and tending to the usual activities of a divine site. At an Asklepieion they had less leisure than those holding similar posts at other sanctuaries, since there was not a single festival date to be observed: the healing sanctuary was always 'open for business'. The members of the chorus at an Asklepieion, who were regularly allotted a portion of any sacrifice, had to sing paeans and offer prayers on an almost daily basis.

They also had to play a role in the dramatic pageants enacted in the evenings, pageants performed to prepare the patients to receive the dreams sent by the god. For an important part of the healing process was the ritual enactment of that process in the theatre. Athenaeus several times reports the action of plays called Asklepios. Actors in plays by Antiphanes and Philetaerus carried out amusing 'cures', while Telestes added music to the script (Edelstein T-611, 613). The latter, indeed, may have played the role of the god in his own dramas as well as those of others, for Suidas lists him as a *komikos*. What was said in these plays has not survived, but many extant stelae show the choristers of the sanctuary in action.

The patients gathered in the public viewing space to watch a pageant performed in the sacred circle before them. The time in the theatre would not be long, for the patients were weak, in pain, and eager to retire to their sleep in the *abaton*. These mini-dramas at the Asklepieia were not the long plays performed for Dionysos each spring in Athens. Not only would the length of the scripts of Athenian dramatists preclude their production at the Asklepieia, but their plots were also unsuitable. For although the Athenian plays are based on familiar myths, patients about to entrust their very lives to healing ministrations – even if from a god – do not want or need to see enacted the tragic fate of Agamemnon or Oidipous. Comedy would be more beneficial, for, as numerous modern studies show, laughter brings many positive effects, but nevertheless a full Aristophanic drama would run far too long. The Asklepieion pageants were composed to be short, symbolic and suggestive.

There is a play based on the events that occurred at an Asklepieion, Aristophanes' *Ploutos* or *Wealth*. In this comedy the scurrilous slave Karion takes the god Wealth to the healing sanctuary to cure his blindness and remains there with him. Upon his return home, the slave tells his master's wife what transpired there: what he did before he retired to the sacred dormitory and what he saw while faking sleep there (652-748). Although his report is enlivened with comic detail, it remains the only literary report extant about the process carried out at an Asklepieion and thus provides a vital link in our understanding of what patients did while within the god's sanctuary. Dodds (1951: 127n.56) offers an important observation about the play:

> But I doubt if the poet intended to hint that the priest of line 676 was identical with 'the god' who appears later. Cario's narrative seems to represent, not what Aristophanes thought actually happened, but rather the average patient's imaginative picture of what went on while he slept.

First, Karion claims, he bathed Wealth in the sea. Then proceeding to the sanctuary, he and his charge watched the sacrificial cakes burnt and noted how oil heightened the flame. Moving to the sacred dormitory, Wealth was made to lie down, and Karion laid out his mat along with the other patients. Then, reports the imposter patient, the temple servant came, put out the lights and told them to

30

go to sleep, and to ignore all noises. So they all lay there quietly 'in rows like herring'.

Aristophanes gives his slave several comic asides describing what he did while awaiting the god's visit. Seeing a pot of soup by the head of an old woman three beds down, Karion moves to get it before the priest does. For, according to Karion, it is the priest and temple attendants who approach and 'heal' the patients. As Karion watches for an opportunity to steal the soup, he sees the priest gathering the goods from the sacred table, 'consecrating them into his knapsack'. While the priests may not have filched the offerings into their knapsacks, we know they did collect the offerings regularly, for it was the offerings that kept the sanctuaries going. In an annual process known as the *kathairesis*, the priests removed the gold and silver ex-votos to be melted down and recast into new cult equipment.[10] Similarly in Greek Orthodox churches and shrines today, the sale of candles is an important addition to their coffers, although an attendant regularly snuffs out the offered candles.

After the priest had passed by, Karion filched the woman's soup; to stop her protests, he hissed and bit her 'like a snake'. The stealing of the soup and Karion's actions are part of the comedy, but his imitation of a snake, closely associated with the god, was appropriate, and within a few lines of his pretence, Karion reports the appearance of actual snakes in the *abaton*.

We do not need to rely upon a comic playwright to ascertain the presence of snakes at Asklepieia; it is well known that the serpent played a part in the healing process. Dream inscriptions from Epidauros report the licking of snakes, Asklepios is portrayed in art, both in painting and sculpture, with an attendant snake, and it is well known that when the Romans suffered a plague in 291 BC, they sent for a sacred snake from Epidauros before they sent for a doctor.[11] Many scholars think that the round maze of the *tholos* at Epidauros was the home of the sacred snake(s). While such an elaborate snake pit (*bothros*) has not been found at the other major sites, a small *bothros* set off in a special chamber at the Asklepieion in Athens is thought to have served to house the sacred serpent.

According to Karion's report, Asklepios himself soon appeared, accompanied by his two daughters, Iaso and Panacea. Faking sleep, Karion watched carefully as the god made his rounds. A slave in attendance on 'the deity' brought forth a mortar and pestle and a medicine box. Grinding up garlic, fig juice, squill and vinegar, the slave made a poultice for the eyes of one Neokleides who had come to the sanctuary to be cured of blindness. When the patient cried out in pain, the god said (according to Karion), 'I thought you liked being plastered.' But when he came to Wealth, the god performed more gentle ministrations: first he wiped his eyes with clean linen, then asked Panacea to wrap a purple cloth around Wealth's head and face. The god then clicked his tongue and two serpents appeared. These slipped beneath the cloth and licked Wealth's eyes – and almost immediately Wealth jumped up, cured of his blindness. The other patients gathered around him, celebrating Wealth's new-found ability to see.

We can imagine similar scenes taking place at any Asklepieion and that the cures witnessed would be reported far and wide. Probably not every patient left the sanctuary cured, but those who did put up the dedications that others saw. In Aristophanes' play, after the celebrations and congratulations, Karion and his healed deity left the god's sanctuary; in real life those who had been healed by the god would have done the same. For the comedy in all its parts is a record of what patients experienced at an Asklepieion. The Athenian audience would have left laughing both at the playwright's humorous lines and at the details they recognized about the events occurring in the sanctuary, either on the basis of their own experience or from what their friends had told them.

Aristophanes clearly indicates that Karion was watching rituals performed by the temple priests and attendants for the patients sleeping in the *abaton*. The people of the sanctuary appeared to these patients in their dreams, repeating a performance they had enacted before bedtime in the theatre of the Asklepieion. Aristophanes' drama within his drama confirmed for his audience their experiences when they visited the healing god, and offers us evidence of what went on during the nights of cure at a sanctuary of Asklepios.

The inter-relationship between pageant and religion is not limited to the performances in the Asklepieion *odeia*. The key elements of the rituals practised at the Eleusinian Mysteries focused upon drama, words and revelation, and there is a close connection between the cult of Asklepios and that celebrated at Eleusis. When the god was first brought to Athens (probably from his sanctuary at Zea in the Peiraeus), he was given 'temporary accommodation' at the Eleusinion in the Athenian Agora. The introduction of the cult coincided with the nine-day Eleusinian festival; the fourth day was later termed *Epidauria* and was designated for those who arrived after the festival had begun. More importantly, several aspects of the Eleusinian ritual were echoed in that of Asklepios. Both had a 'revealer of mysteries', the *hierophantes*; in the Mysteries this was a priest who revealed the holy objects, at an Asklepieion it was the priest who enacted the actions of the god. A drink of honey, wheat, mint and oil was consumed by the initiates at Eleusis in remembrance of Demeter and by the sick at Epidauros in honour of Hygieia, Asklepios' daughter and a goddess of health. Burkert (1985: 268) reports that a piglet was sacrificed at both sanctuaries. Garland (1992: 123-4) suggests that the six male figures greeting the goddesses on a votive relief found at the Athenian Asklepieion are members of the medical profession; I suggest they could be actors in the pre-retirement pageant.[12] Finally, it is generally believed that the rituals culminating the sixth day of the Mysteries at Eleusis involved some type of dramatic performance.

For while the actual events and revelations of the *dromena, legomena* and *deiknymena* of the Eleusinian ceremony (the *teletê*) remain unknown, most scholars agree that the pageant (*dromena*) was an enactment of the abduction and return of Persephone. The site of Eleusis supports this interpretation, with one cave suitable for Hades' seizure of the maiden, the other with its secret stairway and opening for Persephone's return. The text (*legomena*) is as lost to us as any Asklepieion script. However, the many images of wheat, poppies, and enthroned goddesses found within the sanctuary suggest the objects and vision of the final revelation (*deiknymena*). Finally, the Niinnion tablet, now in the museum at Eleusis, shows the procession (*pompê*) to Eleusis. Similar enactments can easily be imagined as part of the rituals for Asklepios, but these would be performed in the sanctuary theatres, since the patients, unlike the initiates, would not be able to wander easily throughout the sanctuary.

In the world of contemporary medicine, patients go to the hospital, either by appointment or by ambulance to the ER. They believe that the doctors there can cure their illness or disease. So did ancient peoples go to the sanctuaries of the god who they believed could offer a release from their suffering. As one has to ask for an appointment today, so the ancient patient had to ask the god for his help. They also had to make an offering as payment to the deity and his priests – a requirement that is also very much a part of the modern medical experience in the American health care system.

How did a patient ask Asklepios for his aid? In all areas of ancient religion, the request was a requirement of the process of seeking a divinity's aid. At Epidauros, it seems it was easy to meet the obligation: the very coming to the sanctuary with sincere belief seems to have been sufficient. But before entering the *abaton*, patients had to go through rites of physical purification, had to offer cakes of honey and cheese, and finally had to watch a sacred pageant in the sanctuary's theatre. After they retired to the *abaton,* the god came to the patients during their sleep within its chambers; during this period of incubation the god answered their requests via the temple dreams.

After Asklepios effected or suggested a cure, post-cure religious ceremonies were a part of the prescribed ritual. Inscriptions and other testimonials make it clear that what the god had said must be done. The patient, of course, was expected to follow the regimens the god (or his priests) had suggested. After the cure, payment must be rendered to the sanctuary attendant and an offering made to the god and his priests. The nature of these offerings is nicely described in Herondas' *Mime* 4, a text I discuss in the next chapter.

Before examining performance and cure for the sick, I think it worthwhile to consider the rituals of thanksgiving which we now might call 'preventative medicine.' Probably everyone included in their daily worship a prayer of thanks for their good health. Anyone who forgot to do so might suffer a bad dream, a warning from the god that the divinity was due some acknowledgement for the good health one enjoyed. The individual so warned could at once offer a sacrifice to Asklepios – a gift that was a form of preventative medicine.[13] The sacrifice to the healing deity did not need to be elaborate; the proverbial 'cock for Asklepios', recorded as Socrates' last words, was generally held to be an adequate offering.

Prayer itself, of course, has healing properties: the one who prays believes that the god hears the prayer and from that belief gains confidence and a feeling of connection. The importance of prayer for healing is not limited to the ancient world. As Fontana and Valente

(1993: 134) suggest, modern studies include the ability to pray as one of the key components of a healthy psyche.

Also included in the practices of maintaining health were the general prescriptions of the priests at the sanctuaries and the doctors in their local clinics, their *iatreia*. Much of the Hippokratic corpus is devoted to the promotion of clean water, fresh air, daily exercise and proper diet, and it would seem that the belief in the importance of these was widespread among the Greeks. Hippokrates opens his discussion in his *On Airs, Waters, and Places* by advising that one should take note of the climate in an area and especially observe the quality of the water. It is important to notice also, he continues, the lifestyle of its inhabitants: what are their pursuits, their habits in drinking and eating (not in excess), and whether they are fond of exercise and work.

When patients were cured, they offered immediate thanks to the deity: if the cure occurred, it clearly happened by the ministrations and will of the god. When thank-offerings, *anathêmata*, were set up, the patients making the dedication were presenting both their own gift of thanks and a lasting testimony to the god's gift. As Burkert (1985: 93) puts it, the *anathêma* is 'a witness to one's relationship to the deity, the principal form of expression for private devotion and the most representative document of official piety... The pious act of dedication is thereby transformed into an act of public ostentation.' The offering could be an animal or money (which the priests certainly appreciated), but simple things served as well: garlands, candles or a treasured garment were acceptable. The patients who entered the *abaton* wore garlands of bay leaves, and these were left for the god. But once healed, many people wanted to leave a more tangible and lasting gift. The most common *anathêmata* at Asklepieia were models of the part of the body that was cured: legs, eyes, arms – archaeology has revealed every part of the human anatomy reproduced in terra-cotta or bronze. Similar dedications are still made at healing shrines today; often the holy icons are almost obscured by the silver or shiny tin representations of body parts, all of which are for sale immediately outside the church, as they must have been at the entrances to the ancient healing sanctuaries.

Because patients wanted, or needed, to seek the god's help at any time, the sanctuary needed to be regularly open; the god would treat all people individually whenever they came. While the usual visitors to the sanctuaries for Asklepios were ill, others not in immediate need of a cure also journeyed to the sanctuary. Among them were those who came to attend the festivals held as part of the religious calendar: Asklepios, as the other deities, had regular festival days. The ancient Greek had as many special dates to observe as does any contemporary Catholic or Greek Orthodox follower. But there was a difference. As Burkert (1985: 215) points out, 'Polis festivals for Asklepios come to be overshadowed by private cult ... Consequently there arises in the Asklepios sanctuary the institution of a daily service of worship, in contrast to the usual alternation of festival and ordinary days.'

The festivals for Asklepios included rituals such as were practised at the sanctuaries for other major deities. At Epidauros there were even athletic contests held shortly after those at Nemea and Isthmia, although they were never part of the Big Four 'Circuit' (*periodos*) and were certainly not associated with the healing rituals taking place in other parts of the sanctuary. It is possible, of course, that family members attendant upon a patient might enjoy the diversion of an athletic spectacle. During the rituals celebrated on the god's festival days the theatres were the site for the usual singing of hymns in honour of the god. Furthermore, it seems that from time to time, medical lectures were presented there; Aelius Aristides tells us about those offered at Pergamon. What distinguished the rites at Asklepieia was the inclusion of a dramatic pageant held in the theatre as part of the regular healing ritual.

The patients who sought a cure at the sanctuaries of Asklepios believed the god would heal them. The power of that belief cannot be doubted nor is it limited to the ancient world. As Jerome and Julia Frank argue (1991[3]: 52), effective psychotherapy today can persuade the modern patient to rekindle hope, enhance mastery, heighten self-esteem, and reintegrate patients with their groups. More significant, perhaps, is the evidence provided from such healing sites as Lourdes in southern France, Santiago de Compostela in Spain, or the Greek island of Tenos.

While miracle cures have occurred throughout time, cures for which no medical explanation can be given, more relevant to the evidence from the Asklepieion experience are contemporary placebo studies. As noted above, a placebo may be defined as anything (whether pill, regime or surgery) prescribed by a doctor that the doctor believes has no medical effect on the patient's (apparent) condition. The placebo effect is the resulting improvement in the patient.

In an article published in the *New York Times Magazine* of 9 January 2000, Margaret Talbot reported several studies in which doctors deliberately used placebos, either pills or procedures, with which patients with a variety of ailments became cured. If the doctors administered pills and advice in a positive and caring manner, the patients would heal. Ethical questions arose: is it right to dupe the patients? Could the patients cope with the idea that their ailment had, indeed, been all in the head? It would seem to depend upon the type of illness. But still, the evidence kept appearing that placebos, while lies, were 'lies that heal'.

The article continued, however, with the suggestion that physician attitude, working with patient belief, was as important in the healing process as the prescribed sugar-pill. Explanations of why placebos work seem to centre upon the atmosphere in which the pills are prescribed:

> What all explanations have in common ... is the element of expectation, the promise of help on the way that can only be imparted by another human being ... Hope can help soften the experience of illness, though it cannot cure the underlying disease ... a compassionate and optimistic physician can be a walking placebo.

The placebo effect does not lie behind all cures which occur without immediate medical care. Many people today who trust in holistic medicine also believe in the power of dreams, considering dreams to be a message from God delivered via the psychosomatic network. Dreams thus give information as to a person's physiological and emotional condition. As Wright and Adams have written (2000: 105), 'People have been listening to dreams since the beginning of time; [in the process] used in the ancient temples of Greece ... priests and priestesses would help the dreamer to prepare for sleep by observing certain rituals which would encourage healing.'

At the ancient Asklepieia, patients were healed, and in the modern clinic, patients recover. At the former site, the cure was prompted by the dramatic ritual in which Asklepios was shown healing a patient. In the latter setting, the outcome is usually attained by medicine, but it may result from a doctor's prescription of a placebo and the way it is prescribed. Drama enacted in a context of true belief can banish illness and restore health, whether in the sanctuary of the god or the office of a caring physician. For in that office the modern doctor reflects the ministrations of the ancient god in playing the role of the benevolent healer. Patients so tended can move more rapidly along the road to healing.

The Evidence

There is a place where knowledge and technique stop and the spirit moves where it wants.

Richard Selzer, *Taking the World in for Repair*, 51

While Aristophanes' comedy *Ploutos* provides the most detailed 'evidence' of what occurred at the god's sanctuaries, there are other accounts of how the deity cured those who came to his Asklepieia. The collection of testimonies by Emma and Ludwig Edelstein (1945/ 1998) shows the wide range and variety of these reports; their exhaustive study provides the greater part of the literary evidence I use here. In addition to texts and inscriptions, there are several carved stelae which clearly present the deity and his patient, showing how he cures by his own touch or that of his serpent. Literature and art offer information about the cures that took place at the ancient Asklepieia.

While we may never know *how* the god cured, we know from modern placebo and PNI studies that disease can respond to an impetus other than medicine. While there are also contemporary reports of 'miracle' cures – which can be neither dismissed nor denied, I think that the more scientific evidence of placebo cures offers a better parallel to what went on at the sanctuaries of Asklepios.

The best evidence for the healing that occurred at the ancient Asklepieia lies in the inscriptions, the *iamata*, set up by the patients who received a cure from the god. Second to these are the literary sources, such as Herondas' fourth *Mime* or the long passages from Aelius Aristides. Finally, the above-mentioned stelae showing the god healing and the *anathêmata* hung up by patients in thanksgiving for their cure prove that those who came to the healing sanctuaries departed in health. The contemporary practice of hanging small images (*tamata*) of the cured body part in churches and at other healing sites confirms the ancient practice: those who believe are cured.

Such thank offerings are not limited to religious sites, places where divinity has touched the patients and healed their ills. At Shands Hospital at the University of Florida, patient-painted tiles lining the Atrium wall and corridor ceilings offer thanks to the doctors and nurses, as well as to God, for the care and cure received during an illness. The desire to express gratitude in this way is clearly the same as in the ancient sanctuary. At Shands, however, the patients themselves paint the tiles under the direction of the artists who work or volunteer in the hospital's Arts-in-Medicine program. Each is a unique personal expression, unlike the ancient *anathêmata* or modern *tamata* which were/are mass-produced to be purchased by those who have been healed.

The extant examples in both art and literature provide information as to the nature of the cures, the sorts of medical problems patients brought to the god, how the sanctuaries functioned, and, finally, that cures did take place. We cannot doubt that evidence even though we may not be able to offer a rational explanation for how the cures occurred. We can doubt that they took place exactly as the dream visions assert – for these are often very strange – but we must accept that the patients are reporting the dream as they experienced it and that the results are as the patients recorded them.

The inscribed stelae (*iamata*) set up at Epidauros offer testimony to all who come to the site that miracle healings have taken place there. The power of suggestion, be it the stelae at the ancient Asklepieia or the reputation of or dedications at such contemporary healing sites as Lourdes, Tenos, Fatima or Santiago de Compostela, is great. Those who come seeking cure and see that others have received the divinity's aid are thus prepared for and indeed expect the god's help. We should not dismiss the *iamata* because the cures seem fantastic, because they served the purpose of telling patients that as others had been cured they, too, could hope the god would come to them. As Teijeiro (1993: 124) so well puts it, 'The believer can expect that divinity will help him in specific moments, over and above natural laws; he can expect and ask for a miracle to be performed.' As each patient receives a cure and sets up a record of it, the suggestive power grows; the curing power of Asklepios was believed for almost a thousand years. What, then, do the *iamata* at Epidauros tell us?

The texts are dedicated to god (*theos*) unspecified, or to Asklepios (Apollo is not addressed) or in what would seem to be a sort of hedging, to Good Fortune (*tychê agatha*). Louise Wells (1998: 22) has identified a four-part formulaic pattern for the inscriptions: the identity and complaint of the patients, that they slept in the *abaton,* the cure they received, and the votive offering they made. The suppliants came to Epidauros from all over the Greek world. The only exception is that none seem to have come to Epidauros from Corinth, an absence that can be explained because there was already a well-established Asklepieion there. Those visitors from Athens may well predate the secure establishment of the god's sanctuary in their home city.

The most common ailment affected the eye: more patients suffered blindness, either partial or complete, from disease or injury, than any other complaint. Eye problems were equally numerous among those who sought the god's help at Athens.[14] While it is possible that there were seasonal airborne causes for these apparently frequent ailments, perhaps the eye was that part of the body most easily cured by the god. Relief did not require surgery, diet, or exercise; a cure could be easily made by a simple application of drugs or poultices. This is the affliction and the cure Karion reports in Aristophanes' *Ploutos*, and this, too, marks the action set out in the comedy as one the audience could immediately recognize. While one dream (*IG* IV^2 A.iv = Edelstein T-423.4) records that the god removed the afflicted eyeball, poured in a drug, replaced it, and thus restored the patient's vision, we need not believe the details of the dream, only the results.

The *iamata* and other written accounts of cures for various ailments and complaints frequently does appear to record that the god accomplished miracles. Nevertheless, while many might have recovered from what we would today call the 'placebo effect', PNI studies confirm the relationship between brain (read belief) and cure. There is sufficient contemporary evidence to allow us to accept the cures related in the *iamata*. While the more extreme dream descriptions are surely spurious, the ability to walk, to eat, to speak against all odds has been documented at Christian sanctuaries; these are medical events which fall within the realm of the probable. For, as has been noted, no limb was ever restored at Lourdes, but general health and a sense of well-being from a visit there are continuously documented. According to a frequently cited *Newsweek* poll conducted in 2000, 84% of Americans believe God performs miracles, and 48% said they had experienced or witnessed one. Faith may outweigh fact in these instances, but patient after patient claims to have been cured. Those who visited the Asklepieia believed the god could and did cure them.

The ancient Greeks, for the most part, eschewed magic. The Hippokratic texts heap scorn upon those who suggested that magic had any part in the cause or cure of epilepsy (*On the Sacred Disease* 2-4). While more recent discoveries on both lead tablets and papyrus indicate a belief in the magic of curses, there seems to be little link between magic and health (Teijeiro 1993: 128).

Nor did the Greeks generally think that illness resulted from a moral failing on the part of the patient. While many traditional cultures, and even some Christians today, seek to find the cause of disease in a patient's actions that had, in some way, angered the gods (or God), the Greeks did not look to a divine cause for an individual's illness. A *miasma* could spread through a community for an individual's wrong, such as the plague Apollo sent upon the Greek troops at Troy because Agamemnon had wronged his priest (*Iliad* I.43-100) or upon the city of Thebes as a result of Oidipous' murder of Laios, but in these instances the stain affects the community, not the individual.[15] Apollo is the deity who will punish with disease, but he does not usually send an illness upon a person because of some moral failing or religious wrong: Agamemnon did not fall ill, Oidipous was in good health. Asklepios never sent illness upon a community or an individual; his task was to cure, and he did so individual by individual.

Finally, the ancient Greeks did not think illness came from evil spirits invading the body or the psyche; they did not think that demons had sent the illness. No deity was called upon for an exorcism of an evil spirit who had brought physical suffering. From the earliest days the Greeks believed there were natural, *rational* causes for disease. Thus it was not to a magician that the patient turned, not to a shaman or spiritual healer. The ancient Greeks who were injured or fell ill turned to Asklepios. As they believed in the god, they believed he could cure them. As Teijeiro (1993: 124) points out, 'The believer can expect that the divinity will help him in specific moments, over and above natural laws; that is, he can expect and ask for a miracle to be performed.'[16]

Holowchak (2002: 153) notes that in none of the extant inscriptions is there a description of the god and he finds this surprising. But it is not surprising. Even laying aside the 'need for terseness' in an inscription (Holowchak: 154), we should not find this omission unusual. There were numerous statues of the deity throughout the sanctuary and these images were consistent: Asklepios was always shown as a gentle, bearded, middle-aged figure, either seated or walking with a stick upon which his serpent coiled. In the stelae he appears the same except that he is portrayed in the act of healing, laying his hands upon the sleeping patient or guiding his serpent to lick a wound. As the actor's costume and mask in the pre-*abaton* pageant would have reflected the statues, the patient would not have taken time to record how the god looked – unless his appearance was different from what was expected. The patients at an Asklepieion believed they would see the god, they saw him, and he appeared and acted in the way they believed he would.

Thus the dreams experienced in religious incubation were consistent with the oneiric structure of Greek cultural belief, i.e., as Holowchak (2002: 162) puts it, 'Oneiric content is determined by the social customs and norms of a people.' What is interesting to note is that the dream visions of the Greeks did not significantly change over time, that is, the dream visions recorded in Homer's texts or fifth-century dramas are similar to those inscribed on the *iamata* at Epidauros in the fourth century BC.

And once the deity had provided a cure, the patient thanked him with an appropriate offering, both immediately after recovering and again at a later date. As commemorative rituals honoured the dead long after a death, so those healed by the god could give him a gift of appreciation in remembrance of their cure. This practice continues today, when flowers are laid at a grave on the anniversary of a death, or thanksgiving prayers are offered to a saint at various dates after health has been restored. A record of such a commemorative action exists in a poem from the Hellenistic period.

As we learn from *Idyll* 15 of Theokritos about the celebration of the festival for Adonis, the *Adonia*, in Alexandria, so we can learn about the Asklepieion on Kos and its rituals from Herondas' fourth *Mime*. While the *Mimes*, like Aristophanes' *Ploutos*, were composed to entertain and amuse, their words usually mocking their contemporary world, the details which Herondas sets out appear to give an honest account of what the visitors to the sanctuary saw and what they offered for whatever cure they had received.

Kynno and Kokkale open the mini-drama by greeting the deity. In Kynno's opening words Herondas seems to cover all options concerning the god's origins:

> Hail, Lord Paieon, you who rule Trikka and dwell between Kos and Epidauros, hail to Koronis who bore you to Apollo ....

She continues by saying she has brought a cock for Asklepios – a small offering as they are not people of substance. But the *Neokoros* (Sacristan) brushes aside her apologies, assuring her the god is fully pleased with the gift. Indeed, the idea that each should give to the god according to his means was standard; Hesiod had first voiced it (*Opera* 336) and Aristides quotes it when offering to the god the speech written in his honour (*Oratio* 42:2-3):

> I am concerned, of course, with gratitude and honour expressed through sacrifices and incense, whether this devotion be offered according to the counsel given by Hesiod, or whether it be more generous than one can afford; but the offering that consists in speeches seems by far the most appropriate for me.

In a manner reminiscent of Theokritos' Gorgo and Praxinoe, Kynno and Kokkale babble on, describing the statues that adorn the sanctuary: young men, a girl reaching for an apple – their description recalls the poems of Sappho and Catullus – an old man, a young boy with a goose – this recalling the Hellenistic statue attributed to Boethos of Chalcedon. They themselves have brought a *pinaka*, a painted tablet which they place on a table next to an image of Hygieia. As they await the opening of the door, Kynno berates their slave girl (again, as does Praxinoe in *Idyll* 15) for not quickly calling the Sacristan, while Kokkale continues the narrative describing the rich offerings displayed within the sanctuary.

43

The women have come to the Asklepieion to thank the deity for a cure they had received. What the god cured they do not say, only that he had 'wiped away their diseases by laying his gentle hands upon them'. Their words reflect the action illustrated in the stelae: the god laying his hands upon a sleeping patient. Their thanksgiving seems to be both earnest and genuine.

As the women prepare to leave, however, the *Mime* turns to comedy: Kynno advises Kokkale to cut off the cock's leg for the Sacristan, give the innards and cakes to the sacred snake, and take the rest to eat at home. The Sacristan protests at this: at least give me some of the sacred bread, he exclaims. The sharing of the sacrificial animal is an essential part of the communion rituals of all Greek cults, and an inscription at Pergamon (Edelstein T-491) asserts that the right leg is the part designated for the god's priests. The protest of the Sacristan here, however, implies that the women have not shared quite enough with the god and his sanctuary's attendants at Kos.

In the ancient world there was not a very wide gulf between the skill of the physician and the advice of the divinity. Physicians honoured Asklepios and were themselves called 'Asclepiads'. The doctor, the *iatros*, repeated the information imparted at the sanctuaries in regard to drugs and diet, and the writings of Hippokrates point out that dreams offer valid information. In *Regimen* (IV.86) it is stated:

He who has learnt aright about the signs that come in sleep will find that they have an important influence upon all things ... When the body is at rest, the soul, being set in motion and awake, administers her own household, and of herself performs all the acts of the body ... [for] the soul when awake has cognizance of all things – sees what is visible, hears what is audible, walks, touches, feels pain, ponders. In a word, all the functions of body and of soul are performed by the soul during sleep. Whoever, therefore, knows how to interpret these acts aright knows a great part of wisdom.

Aristophanes' comedy suggests that the priests deliberately imper-sonated the divinity. However, there is no evidence that they were to be regarded as in some way divine. Rather the priests, acting as the god's representatives, first portrayed the divinity's actions in the

44

ritual pageant and then visited the patients asleep in the *abaton*. In the light of day they helped the patients interpret their dreams; they could also give advice to underscore what the patient believed the god had directed. While many of the cures reported at Epidauros (and elsewhere) appear miraculous, others seem to be based on possible options. From their review of the evidence the Edelsteins write (II.141):

> The medical achievements of Asclepius, then, did not consist solely in his performance of miracles. He was also a scientist; his contribution extended from the discovery of slight medical details to that of whole departments of medicine, even to that of the art itself. This is the typical picture of the patron of a craft ... In turning to an investigation of the divine healing, as it was practised by Asclepius throughout the centuries, one must keep in mind that this god was himself a physician, the protector of medicine, as it was developed by Hippocrates, by Herophilus, by Galen and by many others famous in the history of science.

Inscriptions, literature and art record that people were cured at the ancient Asklepieia. From contemporary research on the cures experienced at healing sanctuaries and the ever-growing number of placebo studies, we know that the power of symbols and rituals has an effect on the patient, and the authority of the physician promotes a positive reaction. As Kinsley (1996: 166) notes, the patient's faith in the doctor 'awakens' the patient's own inner doctor. The doctor's role is to inspire the patients to heal themselves. Oddly, no matter what the healer prescribes, the patient improves. To understand what happened at the ancient sanctuaries of Asklepios, we can replace 'the doctor' in those sentences with 'the god'.

2. The Sanctuaries

Epidauros

At Epidauros ... a man, already made separate by his disease, further withdraws from mankind by entering his dreams, surrendering to their power. It is an encounter with the divine in the natural miracle of healing. At Epidauros each healing was an epiphany of the gods.

Richard Selzer, 'The Surgeon as Priest', 46

The Site: History, Buildings, Influence

The Asklepieion at Epidauros, established in the later years of the sixth century BC, became the primary centre for the cult of the god, the main destination of pilgrimage and the major colonizing site: from here the Asklepieia at Athens, Pergamon and Rome (among others less famous) were founded. At this sanctuary of Asklepios the most famous structure today is its theatre, built by Polykleitos of Argos in the later fourth century BC adjacent to the god's sanctuary. While that theatre is best known in modern times for the festival of dramatic performances held every summer, we can be certain it was not originally constructed for entertainment as the Greeks did not put on dramas for pleasure. The theatre played a part in dream therapy, the process of healing practised at the god's sanctuary. After watching a ritual pageant in the theatre, the patients moved to the *abaton* beside the god's temple, where they slept and awaited the nocturnal visit and healing actions performed by Asklepios or his sacred animals, the serpent or the dog.

The extensive archaeological remains at Epidauros underscore the prominence of this sanctuary of Asklepios. Epidauros is situated several miles from the coast of the Saronic Gulf in the northeastern part of the Argive peninsula. Lying in a valley encircled by Mts Arachnaion, Koryphaion, Kynortion and Titthion, long a place where festivals celebrated the rebirth of nature each spring under the auspices of Apollo, the site was associated with Asklepios by the late sixth century BC. The sanctuary was under the management of the port city of Epidauros, from which a sacred way led to the sanctuary. Most religious sanctuaries, being holy sites and thus banning births and deaths within them, were tended and directed by nearby cities: Elis managed Olympia, the Corinthians directed the ceremonies at Isthmia, and Oropos cared for the sacred Amphiareion. Delphi was unusual in that the annual festival was administered by an amphictyony, a regional association of twelve tribes; nevertheless the nearby Phokians looked after the day-to-day affairs of Apollo's sanctuary.

46

II. Drama and Healing in Ancient Greece

A tour of the site itself deserves our first attention. Epidauros has been extensively excavated over the years and a major reconstruction project was started in the early twenty-first. Archaeological work at the healing sanctuary began under Greek direction in the nineteenth century, at which time most of the remains now to be seen were uncovered. With the exception of the theatre, little stands above ground level, a situation that indicates the systematic destruction of the site.[17]

Ancient visitors entered from the north through the *propylon*, a once-impressive entry gate. Immediately to the left (east) stand the ruins of a large basilical church, probably dating from the fifth century AD, at which it seems the healing cult continued. Its placement is significant: built within the confines of a sanctuary to Christ's most powerful rival (I discuss this rivalry in Chapter IV) the church asserts its new primacy. Its site also offers further confirmation that holy sites remain holy; time and time again the incoming religion builds atop its predecessor, thus at once conquering the earlier deity while taking advantage of any special powers blessing the place.

While the modern visitor to the site enters from the southeast, we can follow the route of the ancient patient or pilgrim to Epidauros, who entered through the Ionic and Corinthian columns of the gateway to the sanctuary. The approach to the *propylon*, like that of other buildings here, is by a ramp, not steps, clearly a concession to the patients who came to seek a cure. First we pass by buildings dating to various periods from classical to Christian times. Here were a Greek fountain house, some Roman baths, and a large portico. In the area between these buildings and the main section of the sanctuary stood numerous statues (of which only the bases remain) and *exedra*, semi-circular marble benches on which to rest and watch other patients walking for their prescribed exercise. Finally we approach the *abaton* and at last face the god's temple.

The temple of Asklepios, a marvel of architecture in its day, exists now only in its foundation courses. Theodotos directed its construction, probably in 380-375 BC. Although it was one of the smallest Doric temples in Greece, having 6 x 11 columns but lacking an interior colonnade or back chamber (*opisthodomos*), nevertheless it was splendid in its material and its adornment. We know about its construction from inscriptions found at the site which are now displayed in the

47

museum there, records which indicate it was a truly expensive temple to build. Black and white stone imported from Corinth formed its patterned floor and precious inlays decorated its interior features. This expensive work was completed within four years and eight months – stiff fines insured that assigned jobs were completed on schedule. External decoration was equally fine, as indicated both by ancient description and extant pieces. On the east (front) pediment 22 figures, male and female, enacted the Sack of Troy, while a battle of Greeks and Amazons adorned the west. The roof sculptures, the *acrotêria*, were especially graceful: a Nike (Winged Victory) stood triumphant in the centre, while personifications of the breezes, Aurai, graced the lateral corners.

Thrasymedes of Paros created the image of Asklepios housed within the temple. Pausanias (II.27.1-2) reports the deity's appearance. The god, made of gold and ivory, like the famous Athena Parthenos in Athens, was seated upon a throne and grasping his staff, with his other hand extended over his sacred serpent, while his dog lay beside him. Although that statue of the divinity has long been lost, a marble copy stands in the site museum, and the numerous images found around the Greek and Roman world consistently reveal Asklepios' appearance. He is portrayed as a kindly god, usually bearded, always with his staff around which the sacred snake twines. As noted earlier, the modern conception of Asklepios' staff with twin serpents rising at its top is not ancient at all, but developed from a misunderstanding of classical mythology, an interpretation which blended the heraldic wand (*caduceus*) of Hermes with the walking staff of the healing god.

Immediately in front of the temple, slightly off axis, is the altar, the most essential part of any sanctuary. As visitors to ancient sites today, we can easily overlook this fact, as altars are usually the first item to vanish from a sanctuary, for freestanding well-cut blocks are easily moved for reuse in other structures. While in many sanctuaries the altar would pre-date the temple, at Epidauros it seems the temple came first. Adjacent to the sacred boundary wall, the *temenos*, of the Asklepios temple stood a small temple to Artemis, again, poorly preserved. It once had ten interior Corinthian columns and the unusual feature of gutter spouts in the shape of dog heads, probably in honour of the sanctuary's canine healer.

Second in importance to the temple of the healing divinity was the

48

abaton in which the patients slept. Here they awaited the dream visions of the god and/or his daughters or sacred animals. The structure had two sections, a single story on the east, and two levels on the west. Twenty-nine Ionic columns along the south-facing front supported the roof, while the interior was divided into sleeping chambers. A fountain house, requisite for ritual (and personal) bathing, abutted the west end of the *abaton*; the tablets recording the miracle cures experienced by patients at Epidauros were discovered in its well. When the reconstruction of the *abaton* is finished, it will offer the first standing example of this key structure of every healing sanctuary.

The most unusual structure at Epidauros is the *tholos* or, as the round building is sometimes termed, the *thymelê*.[18] Each and every Asklepieion naturally included within its area a temple to the healing god, some type of stoa or portico to serve as an *abaton*, and a space for viewing a pageant presentation. The *tholos* with its elaborate and mysterious design is (to date) unique to Epidauros, although at Pergamon there is a simple round building in the Asklepieion.

Any round building may be termed a *tholos*, and there are several notable ones at well-known sites. Best known (and also mysterious in purpose) is that in the lower sanctuary at Delphi. Most significant for site identification is the *tholos* in the Athenian agora, for its discovery gave an orientation to the archaeologists of the American School of Classical Studies at Athens when they began excavating the ancient marketplace. An historically important *tholos* (but often overlooked) stands within the *temenos* at Olympia, put up by Philip of Macedon to celebrate his domination of Greece.

The Epidaurian *tholos*, standing to the south just behind the temple, was exquisite in its external design and singular in its interior construction. Beneath the building its architect created a labyrinth of six concentric circles, each with a door and a transverse wall, forcing anyone walking its circuit to complete each circle and reverse direction. Polykleitos, architect of the theatre, was said to have created the lavish style and adornment of the outer building, which inscriptional records show cost two times more than the expensive temple to Asklepios. A ring of Doric columns formed the external ring and a circle of Corinthian columns made an interior colonnade around the open labyrinth. Atop the conical roof stood an elaborate and beautiful acanthus. Each marble ceiling tile within blossomed with an intricately carved flower, while the walls sported panels painted by Pausias. The floor was patterned with black limestone from Argos and Pentelic marble from Athens. All in all, this *tholos* took pride of place among ancient structures for its beauty. The reconstruction plans for Epidauros mentioned above include the rebuilding of the *tholos* so that its ancient appearance may again be visible to the site's visitors.

The purpose of the *tholos*, however, is entirely unknown. No ancient source describes its use. Although Epidauros has more inscriptional evidence for its buildings than most sites (only the Athenian Akropolis has more), and although the architect and the cost of the *tholos* are known, its function is not. Speculation most consistently offers two possibilities. Some say that the sacred serpent(s) of the god were kept within the labyrinth and let out at night to visit the patients sleeping in the *abaton* directly across from it. Others say that the *tholos* was dedicated to the chthonic or underground aspect of Asklepios, counterpart to his Olympian status celebrated in the temple. I argue that both interpretations are valid. The *tholos* represented the chthonic aspects of the god and could serve as a home for the sacred serpents. According to his myth, the healing divinity had been blasted to the realm of the dead by the lightning of Zeus and then restored to earth to carry on his ministrations. The serpents represented the chthonic Asklepios. And although worthy of a temple like any Olympic god, Asklepios did not ascend to Mt Olympus but remained on earth among mortals. His legend was unlike that of any other deity nor did he act as did other divinities, but he was equally worthy of recognition and veneration. As sacrifices appropriate to the gods of the upper world were not suitable for those of the dead, so Asklepios, chthonic and Olympian deity, required a separate venue for the two realms he represented. And as the dual aspects of this god had equal importance, each required an equally significant and beautifully designed sacred space. Finally, the triangle formed by temple, *tholos* and *abaton* formed a second setting for the rituals celebrated for the god and the healing rites performed by him.

Moving southwest from the *tholos* the visitor would pass by a square altar to Apollo, first inhabitant of the site, the unidentified (but apparently important) 'building E' and the small temple to Artemis. Turning further southwest, one arrives at a large square building enclosing a porticoed courtyard in which the Romans built a small *odeion*. This complex was as important to the sanctuary as were the ritual triangle and the theatre.

On older plans the structure is identified as a gymnasium with an interior *palaestra* (wrestling arena) and it does bear some resemblance to that building at Olympia. However, a closer study of the interior rooms revealed that these were not exercise or lecture rooms but rather dining rooms, and thus more recent site plans label this building as an *estiatorion*, a dining hall. Its central courtyard would have been the scene of rituals, not wrestling, a place of communal offerings to the god, a place of prayers for healing and thanksgiving for cures. It is instructive that the Romans built an *odeion* within that space, thus continuing its original purpose, now in Roman form. Perhaps this alteration in the spatial arrangement of the building allowed participants at the god's rituals to better see the pageant, perhaps this became a place for patients to view the dramatic pageants of the cult in a more private setting.[19] They would also be closer to the temple and *abaton*, and thus have a shorter walk before they slept.

Finally, en route from the healing sanctuary proper to the grand theatre, the visitor would see a *katagôgion*, a hotel, which once stood two stories high and had 160 rooms around four colonnaded courtyards. A Greek bath (as distinguished from Roman *thermae* to the north) stood just beyond the hotel. It is unusual that it lay within the *peribolos*, the boundary, of the sanctuary; perhaps its placement indicates that this is where patients took their first requisite purifying baths. The sacred area of Epidauros is large, encompassing everything from the *propylon* on the northern boundary and the grand theatre on the south – Pausanias asserts that the theatre is within the holy area. Its inclusion within the *peribolos* underscores the fact that what went on at the theatre was as much a part of the healing ritual as were the other nocturnal preparations.

The theatre draws visitors today to Epidauros. Built into the hillside of Mt Kynortion at some distance below the much older sanctuary to Apollo Maleatas, it was one of the finest in Greece and remains the best preserved of any. Polykleitos gave the theatre a magnificent design, as celebrated in antiquity as it is now for its attractive shape and excellent acoustics. The original design had 34 rows of seats, but a second tier was added in the second century, thus accommodating

14,000 spectators. Whatever rites and pageants were performed in this theatre, each and every word of the actors would have been clearly heard. All Greek theatres had good acoustics, but Epidauros, as the best-preserved theatre, stands extant as the most famous in which to test that acoustical quality.

The perfect round of the orchestra lies tangential to the slightly longer rectangle of the stage. The *parodoi*, side entrances to the acting space, pass through tall and elaborately decorated doorways. Still marked at the orchestra's centre is the place for an altar. At theatres used for festival performances in honour of Dionysos, the altar served as the site for sacrifices to that god, then could be left or removed as necessary for the play's action. Here at Epidauros, the altar was used for sacrifices to Asklepios, the site's resident deity.

Epidauros also boasted a stadium, built adjacent to the sanctuary, and, further away, a hippodrome; the former has been excavated while the latter has not. The stadium's starting lines and the entrance to an underground passage for the athletes are preserved. As at Olympia and Nemea, the sight of the competitors bursting into the arena would offer the same dramatic excitement as does the team emerging into the modern football stadium from the locker rooms beneath the stands. Although the games at Epidauros never reached the status of the four on the Circuit, they were held for centuries. Scheduled shortly after the games at Isthmia, the Epidaurian contests easily drew the athletes and perhaps some of the spectators who had participated in those near Corinth. The festival also included artistic contests, as we learn from the conversation between Socrates and Ion (Plato *Ion* 530A), where the young boy reports that he won first prize in the rhapsodic contest. These may have been held in the theatre or perhaps in the stadium as they were at Delphi. The festival contests, then, not dramatic performances in the theatre would have diverted the attention of those who accompanied the patients to Epidauros as well, of course, as those who came solely as spectators of the various agonistic events.

All in all, the sanctuary for Asklepios at Epidauros was one of the most elaborate in Greece, a site for a healing cult practised in strikingly attractive buildings; it included a magnificent theatre and comfortable accommodations for those who came seeking the god's cure. The Asklepieion lay adjacent to a stadium and hippodrome for athletic contests which would entertain both sports fans and those attendant on the patients seeking the god's cure. Unlike other major sanctuaries, used only for special events, an Asklepieion was in constant use, welcoming a steady stream of patients to its verdant atmosphere. The Sanctuary for Asklepios at Epidauros set the standard for healing centres as the cult spread throughout the Greek and Roman world.

Other Major Healing Sites

Here the god was worshipped. Here, as at other sanctuaries, the spirit of the land combined with ritual practice, faith and urgent need to call the god into the dreams of those seeking healing.

Edward Tick, *The Practice of Dream Healing*, 72

Epidauros is just one healing site with a theatre. Nearly 300 sanctuaries to Asklepios once existed throughout the Greek world; for about half of these some archaeological evidence remains. The sanctuaries were always established in healthful sites with springs of water at hand. Indeed Vitruvius suggests (*On Architecture* 1.2.7 = Edelstein T-707) that it is the site as well as the deity which contributes to the healing at these sanctuaries. He writes:

For when sick persons are moved from a pestilent to a healthy place and the water supply is from wholesome fountains, they will recover more quickly. So it will happen that the divinity from the nature of the site will gain a greater and higher reputation and authority.

While a healthful well-watered site is surely one part of the healing process at an Asklepieion, the deity does more than bask in the shared value of his site's atmosphere; the buildings of his sanctuary are important to his cult. As we examine the sanctuaries with more extensive remains, we find that a theatre or an *odeion* forms part of the site or stands adjacent to it. It is clear the Greeks considered theatres an essential component of a healing sanctuary. As we took a tour of Epidauros, so a tour of some of the better-known and better-preserved healing centres is in order here.

Pergamon

The city of Pergamon stood high above the Caicus River in western Asia Minor. Although not originally a Greek city, it was a healing sanctuary as early as Homeric times and so identified in the epic texts. For when Aineias was wounded in battle, Apollo snatched him away to Pergamon where Artemis and Leto healed his wounds (*Iliad* V.445-8). In time, probably in the late 400s BC, Asklepios would arrive and the Greek god would change the city's destiny forever.

The city's history is rich, but here only a brief review of its Hellenistic period is needed. After Alexander's death, Thrace and western Asia Minor first came into the hands of Lysimachos. He deemed Pergamon, then a mere citadel, worthy of enhancement and under his direction buildings arose at the site. The enhancement of Pergamon continued under the city's next rulers Seleuceus, Antiochus and Eumenes; succeeding kings followed suit until Pergamon became one of the most prosperous and architecturally attractive of the Hellenistic urban centres. It retained much of its Greek character even after Roman conquest.

Atop the hill were the homes of the ruling kings, modest compared to those at Macedonia or Alexandria, but with a commanding view across the plains. A temple to Athena, protector of the city, shared the heights with the kings: divinity and mortal ruler looked out for Pergamon from its highest point.

Immediately below the summit a spectacular steeply raked theatre was built into the western hillside. The auditorium (*cavea*) boasts three seating sections rather than the usual two. The actors on stage must have appeared very small indeed, but good acoustics and the impressive view across the western plain would have been compensation for the visual limitation. Of the many other buildings comprising the urban centre of Pergamon, only two need recognition here: the altar of Zeus and the library. Today mere foundations mark the location of either at the site and the library no longer exists, but the German archaeologists excavating at Pergamon moved the altar piece by piece to Berlin.[20] Fully reconstructed, it stands there as the centrepiece of the Pergamon Museum, although signs in the modern Turkish city of Bergama demand the altar's return. The library deserves note because it was there that parchment replaced papyrus and the codex book replaced the scroll. For when Alexandria put a ban on papyrus, the librarians at Pergamon found a new substance, parchment, and changed the shape of the book forever.

A sanctuary of Asklepios was developed outside the city walls. The healing centre began as a private dedication established *c.* 400 BC, according to Pausanias (II.26.8), by Archias, a local citizen who had been cured at Epidauros. The sanctuary became part of the state cult in the late third century and immediately flourished, especially when Galen took up residence there. For the modern reader, however, Aelius Aristides, the extravagant hypochondriac who spent thirteen years at the sanctuary, remains the best guide to the site and what took place at it. Whatever buildings were within its area during the Hellenistic period, when Attalos III ceded Pergamon to Rome in 133 BC the existing structures were replaced one by one with finer Roman ones, buildings so fine as to earn the sanctuary occasional listing as a 'wonder of the world'.

The wide, paved and colonnaded Sacred Way, the Via Tecta, links sanctuary and town. A marble *propylon* with four Corinthian columns, once topped by an elegant Nike, welcomes the visitor into a rectangular plaza, bordered on north, west and south by Ionic-columned marble stoas. Added to the east side of the sanctuary in the early years of the first century AD is a round temple dedicated to Zeus Asklepios, sometimes identified as Asklepios Soter (saviour). Seven statue niches were provided within, with the image of Zeus Asklepios standing directly across from the entrance. This unusual and elaborate building was privately funded by one L. Cuspius Pactumeius Rufinus, probably at the time of Hadrian. Thus some say its design was based on the Pantheon at Rome, and time and style certainly look to the Pantheon as the inspiration. But another possibility might be considered, the *tholos* of Epidauros. If that round building was a form of temple, not merely a home for the sacred snake, the decision to erect a round sacral space for the healing god at Pergamon might well have been influenced by the building at Epidauros.

To the west of the temple in the centre of the sanctuary lie a series of fountains and sacred springs set off in attractive basins; water still flows to them. The power of this water may have been magical; Aristides asserts it had a wonderful taste. The long-term patient wrote an oration to the well of Asklepios (*Oratio* XXXIX = Edelstein T-804) in which he claims that whoever drinks of its waters 'will think he has tasted Homer's lotus'. From these wells an underground passage (*cryptoporticus*) leads diagonally southeast to the *abaton/enkoimetêrion*, the sleeping and treatment hall. At Pergamon this building is also round, once at least two stories high; its sleeping bays are large, opening off a broad hall that runs the circuit of the building.

On the northwest corner of the sanctuary stands a small *odeion* with a capacity of *c.* 3,500, reconstructed to elegance today. Its inclusion and placement within the Asklepieion indicates that it was a necessary part of the sanctuary. A theatre dominates the upper city of Pergamon, as we have seen, and a second Roman theatre stood near the gymnasium in the lower city. Clearly this small performance space was created for rites and rituals appropriate to Asklepios. The space could also have others uses, of course; Aelius Aristides reports that lectures and hymns were frequently presented in the *odeion*.

The design of the Asklepieion at Pergamon well suggests the interrelationship between the incubation chamber and the theatre. After viewing a healing pageant at the theatre the patients, taking a drink or a brief cleansing at the sacred spring as they passed by, descended to the *cryptoporticus* and proceeded at once to the incubation hall. Who could doubt that the dream visitations offering cures came directly from the deity whose rites they had just seen and whose uniquely round temple stood immediately above the passageway and adjacent to the *abaton*? Within the *temenos* of the Pergamene Asklepieion, as at Epidauros, the separate structures formed a unified whole for the healing process.

Kos

The site most closely associated with healing in antiquity is, of course, the island of Kos, the home of the 'Father of Medicine', Hippokrates. Here, we are told, the patient received treatment from an *iatros*, a doctor. Those who did not believe in dream therapy but wanted the latest in medical care went to see the physicians trained under Hippokrates. People went to Kos in antiquity as today they might go to a healing spa or a leading medical centre.

The association between Asklepios and the healers of Kos remains ambiguous. As John Bowman writes (1992: 59-60):

II. Drama and Healing in Ancient Greece

At Kos the cult overlapped the importance assigned to the island's native son, Hippokrates; he may have been little more than one of the Asklepiadai, or priest-doctors, but he seems to have imposed his own approach to healing on the Asklepieion of Kos.

Inscriptional evidence ascertains that patients were given treatments along lines laid down by Hippokrates. These included regimens of diet, fresh air and exercise, as well as the administration of drugs and the practice of surgery. These treatments, one must note, were very similar to those given at an Asklepieion – with the exception of surgery, perhaps, as any surgical procedure received at a healing sanctuary seems to have been done only in a patient's dream.

Even on Kos, however, the power of the deity could not be ignored; after all, the healing god was originally (and always) a physician. Thus a fine sanctuary to Asklepios stood on the island of Hippokrates. The cult was spread to Kos from Epidauros by the Asklepiadai, a fraternity of priest-doctors who brought a sacred snake from Epidauros to the new sanctuary. There the cult had its own festivals, hymns, processions and sacrifices such as those described in the fourth Mime of Herondas.

The sanctuary of Asklepios on Kos was not built until after the death of Hippokrates, but we do not know if the delay was because of medical or financial reasons. We do know it became a wealthy site in the Hellenistic period under the support of the Ptolemys; Ptolemy Philadelphus was born on the island, and tradition says Cleopatra stored some of her treasure there.

The Asklepieion lies about four kilometres from the ancient town in a sanctuary once sacred to Apollo Kyparessios; as at Epidauros the fame of the son soon eclipsed that of his father at the site. Archaeological excavation of the sanctuary began under the Germans in the early twentieth century, and was continued by the Italians. Originally the sanctuary contained only a temple and an altar, but during the Hellenistic period it was developed to encompass four terraces. On the lower level porticos surround the sacred space on three sides; probably the festivals for Asklepios were celebrated here. The fourth side of the area forms the wall of the next terrace, with a fountain (still functioning) in the centre. On the right of this middle terrace stands an Ionic

57

temple, once adorned with frescoes by Apelles but which Augustus took to Rome. The various rooms for the sick opened onto the third level portico. A great altar rises in front of the temple, complete with a staircase and with columns along its porticoes, in which stood statues of Asklepios and his family. A Roman temple stood to the left of the great altar.

Behind the altar a grand staircase ascends to the upper terrace, where the temple to Asklepios dominates the space. Black and white limestone highlighted this Doric temple. On clear days the view from the upper terrace is vast: one can see Kalymnos to the northwest and to the east, the Turkish coast at Bodrum (site of the Mausoleum) and to the south, Knidos.

The requisite theatre at Kos is not within the sanctuary itself. But an *odeion* stands nearby, an easy walk along (currently) shaded avenues. Since there was a city theatre at Kos the placement of the small viewing space must have been dictated by its proximity to the Asklepieion. As the processional way led from the city centre to the sanctuary of Asklepios at Pergamon, so patients coming to the Asklepieion at Kos could conveniently walk to the healing site. There was, however, a major difference between the treatments received at Kos and those dispensed at Epidauros and other healing sites: at Kos the doctor, the *iatros*, provided the cure, at Epidauros it was the god. Dream therapy mingled more openly with medical care on the island of Kos. Thus the island, home of Hippokrates and site of an important sanctuary to Asklepios, is a vibrant reminder that physician and god shared the medical treatment available to the ancient Greek citizen.

A final note about the island's history could be added, for the tradition of the island as a medical centre did not fade with the passage of time. Although Kos continued to prosper during Roman times, during the sixth century AD the Asklepieion was abruptly devastated, whether by earthquake or vandals is not known. But in the fourteenth century the Knights of St John came to the island and used stones harvested from the Asklepieion to build their castle. The Knights were first established to offer medical care and they continued to honour their original obligation on Kos. And the tradition continues: in the late twentieth century the people of Kos began to restore the ancient site and establish an international medical centre on the island, thereby keeping the healing arts of Hippokrates and Asklepios alive.

Local legend also keeps the island's history alive: guidebooks to Kos assert that the plane tree at its centre is the 'Very Plane Tree of Hippokrates' under which the father of medicine taught his followers. While this is an impressive tree with branches spreading some 100 metres, it is probably at most 500 years old. The columns and piles of ancient marble supporting those branches certainly predate the tree; these, not the tree, probably heard the words of Hippokrates and the dreams recounted by the patients who slept in the island's Asklepieion.

Regional Sites

Hope is the elevating feeling we experience when we see – in the mind's eye – a path to a better future. True hope has no room for delusion.   Jerome Groopman, *The Anatomy of Hope*, xiv

Epidauros, Pergamon and Kos are three of the most famous sanctuaries dedicated to Asklepios. But there are still others of which substantial remains exist, a sort of second tier of significant Asklepieia. These include Corinth, Dion, Messene, Oropos and, of course, the god's healing centre at Athens. Beyond these are the hundreds of Asklepieia identified by Pausanias and Strabo. While for the lesser sites I provide merely a brief discussion, I think it is important to offer here a tour of the four 'second tier' Asklepieia as well as the important sanctuary in Athens.[21] I discuss these sites in alphabetical, not chronological order; the similarity in what makes up an Asklepieion becomes evident from their archaeological remains.

Corinth

Corinth was established on the narrow isthmus that links the Peloponnese to Central Greece and took advantage of its geographical position. Early in its history the rulers and citizens of Corinth set up a way for merchants to transport their cargo from east to west, from the Saronic Gulf to the Gulf of Corinth and thence to western Greece without the dangers and distance of sailing around the southern Peloponnese. This 'ship-railroad', the *diolkos*, enabled those involved in maritime commerce to unload their cargo into carts, raise their ship on to wheels and have both dragged along the track to the other side of the isthmus. Naturally the Corinthians charged fees for all parts of this process, and Corinth became a very wealthy city, as well as one greatly enjoyed by the crews of these vessels. 'It is always fair sailing when one sails to Corinth' was a standard saying.

In addition to the temples – especially the magnificent one to Apollo, impressive with its monolithic columns, and that to Aphrodite tended by 1,000 temple prostitutes, its elaborate stoas and fountain houses, Corinth also boasted a fine Asklepieion. As at other cities, there was apparently a sanctuary to Apollo originally at the site, but by the fifth century BC the healing son supplanted his father as the reigning deity.[22]

The Asklepieion is located in the northwest part of the city, just within the city wall, close by the Lerna stream and not too distant from the theatre and *odeion*. The sanctuary at Corinth is different from those at other sites, both in layout and in what aspects of the cult have been preserved there. Archaeology has recovered neither *iamata* recording a patient's cures nor stelae showing the deity providing them. What the site at Corinth has contributed to the information about the deity's healing powers are numerous *anathêmata*, the anatomical ex-votos that patients hung in thanksgiving to show what part of their body Asklepios had cured. The practice of offering such souvenirs of a cure continues at churches of healing saints today, where the terracotta offerings once hung for Asklepios are repeated in silver or tin at such sites as Tenos and Patmos as well as at a chapel to the healing saints at Corinth itself. The tradition of giving a descriptive thank-offering has never died.

The Asklepieion at Corinth is small relative to those at the other first and second-tier sanctuaries. It consists of just one multi-roomed building adjoining the Lerna springhouse. Several paths led from the town and the theatre areas to the sanctuary, a distance of less than a half a mile. The patient entered the complex through a gateway in the southeast wall. The layout of the sanctuary provided the entrant a three-quarter view of the altar and temple, the layout preferred by the Greek site designer.[23] Immediately to the left of the entry gate was a water basin for initial purification; to the right stood the great altar and the temple to Asklepios behind it. Its high porch required a central ramp over the steps; ramped entryways to assist the sick and infirm are common at Asklepieia. Large square cuttings on either side of the temple probably held the sacred serpents.

The *abaton* lies directly behind the temple. It was constructed so as to take advantage of the Lerna court and fountain: apparently Lerna was a place to which people came for a pleasant outing as well as functioning as part of the healing procedures. The layout of Lerna included dining facilities that reflected those at the *estiatorion* at Epidauros, for the floors show that there were couches and tables in the encircling rooms while cooking was done in the centre court.

A patient arriving at Corinth might initially bath in the nearby waters of the Saronic Gulf, then advance to the spring chambers adjoining the *abaton* for further requisite purification. If the rituals at Corinth were like those at other Asklepieia, patients would see a pageant at the theatre, or more probably at the *odeion* which lies closer to the sanctuary, then follow the path to the cult centre and enter by the southeast gate noted above. After making offerings of honey-cakes and possibly a cock to the god, the patients would retire to their beds and the customary rituals would begin: the lights would be put out and as the patients drifted off to sleep and dream, the god would appear to administer potions or advise a curative action. Whether it was dream or actual therapy, upon awakening the patient would dedicate in joy a terracotta replica of the cured limb or organ. These dedications also show the patients' desire to demonstrate to others the cure the god granted, very much as people today want to tell family and friends about their experiences in the medical arena, what they experienced during their time in the hospital.

Corinth preserves more such terracotta testimonials than any other site. The numbers of body parts recovered, intact or able to be restored, are nothing short of amazing. Archaeological reports assert that over 75 limbs and 110 body parts, in addition to ears and eyes have been catalogued. Within the impressive and wide variety of dedications some medical cataloguing has been done. Patients who came to Corinth had fewer eye complaints than those seeking cure at Epidauros or Athens, but to judge from the number of legs and foot parts (44) they apparently had many more podiatric ailments.

Once their limbs had been repaired the patients could recover their strength in the colonnaded courtyard immediately to the west of the *abaton*. While they would not necessarily return to the city centre, their family members might do so to shop at Corinth's large commercial stoas and drink at the city's many taverns.

61

Dion

Dion, a town in Pieria, lies in the shadow of Mt Olympus in northern Greece and is known for its many sanctuaries: its citizens seemed to have worshipped deities from Greek, Egyptian and Near Eastern cults. According to Pausanias (IX.3), tradition puts the death of Orpheus here. Dion was a town which held many festivals and celebrations. History records King Archelaos as the ruler who brought the town into prominence by instituting a drama festival in honour of Zeus and the Muses and a northern set of Olympic Games; he wished to have a Macedonian equivalent of the Greek theatre and athletic festivals for Dionysos and Zeus. Probably Euripides' *Bacchae* was first staged at Dion's theatre and Philip celebrated his destruction of Olynthus at Dion, rather than in Pella or Vergina. Before setting off for his Persian campaign, Alexander held a nine-day festival in the shadow of Mt Olympus. After the death of Alexander, the Antigonids kept the city prosperous, and later Roman governors followed suit. But after being sacked in the barbarian invasions in the fourth century AD, Dion lay abandoned until the twentieth century.

While Dion's archaeological history begins with a description by W.M. Leake, who visited the area in 1806 and identified several structures, actual excavations began in 1928 under Greek direction and these are still in progress. For many years flooding prevented work over much of the area, but recent drainage has allowed digging to continue, and since 1973 archaeologists have revealed extensive remains from the city's entire history.[24]

In addition to being a city with all the common urban elements, including a theatre built into an artificial embankment and featuring a tunnel running from the stage to the centre of the orchestra (a 'ladder of Charon'), an *odeion*, and a stadium, Dion, appropriate to its name (and as noted above) has numerous sanctuaries, sites holy to a wide variety of divinities. As is to be expected, there is a Sanctuary of Zeus which extends south of the city wall. On the western side of the city, inscriptional evidence as well as an abundance of statuary indicates that cults of Dionysos (adjacent to the theatre), Athena and Kybele were celebrated at Dion. A large and well-defined sanctuary of Isis lies across the stream to the East. On the east side of the city's main road, excavations have brought to light an extensive sanctuary of Demeter, with elements which copy those of Eleusis; to date this is the earliest sanctuary to Demeter found in Macedonia. Evidence of the cults of Baubo, Artemis, Hermes and the Muses has also been uncovered.

There is also an Asklepieion. Its identification was confirmed when a statue of the healing god and members of his family were found within it: portrait statues of Asklepios and his daughters Panakeia and Hygieia graced these halls. Dion's healing centre was designed as part of the Great Baths, or perhaps incorporated into them. Some ten sets of baths have been found at the site, but the Great Baths are the most magnificent. Within these *thermae*, on the right of the Great Hall, were rooms dedicated to the cult of Asklepios.

Also within the bath complex and adjacent to cult rooms of Asklepios stands a small *odeion*. It backs against the agora, so public meetings could be held there; within the baths it could serve as a place for lectures or poetry readings. But it would also have been used as a part of the rituals of Asklepios. As noted above, Dion has a large theatre associated with the cult of Dionysos, and for lectures or concerts an attractive Roman *odeion* lies to the south near the sanctuary of Zeus. When we note that the Great Baths at Dion are the only ones in which there are both a sanctuary for Asklepios and an *odeion*, the linking of the two appears to be a deliberate choice. The cult required a space for the patients to assemble. When so gathered those who came for healing viewed a pageant designed to promote the process.

Messene

Messene (Ithome) is situated in the southwestern Peloponnese and was probably established at the same time and for the same reasons as Megalopolis: to form part of a defence against Spartan aggression. Pausanias (IV.31.5ff.) described the town in great detail: he walked from its amazing walls to its marketplace, thence to its Asklepieion, going on to the theatre, gymnasium and stadium, and finally departing by the Arcadian gate. The location of the city Pausanias so thoroughly reports was never unknown, but as much of it lies under the modern village of Mavromati, little besides its walls was visible on the east, and the ruins of the theatre, stadium and a temple to the west and southwest of the modern settlement. Excavations in the early 1900s uncovered a large square which on the basis of its size and elegance was first thought to be the Agora. But the archaeological work begun in 1957 by Anastasios Orlandos revealed the square's true identity: it was the sanctuary of Asklepios described by Pausanias.[25] Inscriptional evidence and named statuary confirmed the identification and the presence of a small theatre on the northeast corner of the square completes the identity.

The Asklepieion at Messene is large and impressive. It consists of an extensive court, enclosed by stoas on all sides and enhanced by an internal colonnade. In the centre of the north-south axis and facing east stands the god's temple. Its present foundations and Doric elements date from the Hellenistic period, thus indicating a rebuilding of a previous fourth century temple. Immediately to the east the altar is still in situ – unusual for, as noted earlier, altars seldom remain beyond the destruction of a site as these well-shaped easily accessible blocks are an easy temptation to builders who no longer care for the ancient deity.

Several doors pierced the rear walls of the enclosing stoa, offering access to the rooms associated with the cult of the god. Five such rooms lie on the west, with the northernmost formed into a small temple for Artemis Orthia. A bench-lined room on the south has recently been identified as a library; while not universally present, libraries have been discovered at other Asklepieia.

At the north end of the eastern stoa, marked off by a *propylaea*, stands a small theatre. At Messene a space devoted to performances was considered a requisite part of the sanctuary. It lies parallel to the god's temple and near at hand, enclosed within the *temenos* of the sanctuary as at Pergamon. As the remains of another theatre have already been located elsewhere at the site, we can be sure that the one within the Asklepieion played a role in the cult of the god.

Oropos – Amphiareion

Situated between Rhamnous and Delion opposite Eretria, some 31 miles north of Athens, its geography earned the city of Oropos a chequered history. As it lay virtually on the border between Attika and Boiotia, both Athens and Thebes tried to control Oropos, and control over it passed back and forth as the fortunes of Athens and Thebes rose and fell, a conflict noted by Pausanias as still current in his day (I.34.2). Each city-state wanted access to the sea, and archaeology has revealed several ancient harbour installations along the coast.

The present site of Skala Oropou stands on the ancient town of Oropos.[26] It is of interest here because three kilometres to the north lay the sanctuary and oracle of Amphiaraos. The cult was established there in the late fifth century BC; some date its founding to the years between 421 and 415, others place it as late as 411. During the next three centuries Oropos flourished as a place to receive oracles and to seek healing and it remained important until it faded from significance in the fourth century AD. In time earth and vegetation covered the Amphiareion.

Mythology records that Amphiaraos, from whom the sanctuary got its name, was a descendant of the healer and seer Melampos and a king of Argos at the time Polyneikes, son of Oidipous, was gathering an army to march against Thebes. Knowing that the expedition was doomed to death, Amphiaraos did not wish to go. But Polyneikes, using the magical necklace of Harmonia, bribed his wife Eriphyle to coerce her husband into joining the expedition. When the forces of Polyneikes fell at the seven gates of Thebes, Amphiaraos fled; just before he was to fall beneath the sword of his pursuer, Zeus opened the earth with a thunderbolt, receiving the hero and his chariot (and charioteer) into the realm of the dead. The site of his miraculous disappearance became a place of veneration, the locus of a hero cult, the Amphiareion at Oropos.

Perhaps through the hero's relationship to Melampos or perhaps because he had been seized into the earth and thus became associated with Asklepios, the Amphiareion functioned primarily as a healing sanctuary. Patients desiring a cure came to the sanctuary and performed carefully prescribed rites and rituals, observances known from inscriptions and stelae found there. The healing process, as it did at Epidauros and other sanctuaries of Asklepios, relied upon dream therapy. Pausanias asserts (I.34.5) that the hero had initially set up a 'dream oracle', which in time became a healing site. Here, however the incubation ritual was rather different: unlike at Epidauros, the patient had to sleep on the skin of the ram he had just sacrificed to the deity. Gold or silver coins were tossed into the sanctuary spring as payment for receiving the god's word. *Anathêmata* purchased at shops near the stream were also offered in thanks for a cure. Displayed in and around the temple, these reliefs, statuettes and miniatures of cured body parts stood as evidence to all future visitors seeking a way back to health that the resident hero had the power to heal.

The Amphiareion at Oropos is rich with inscriptions. From these we learn the rules of the rituals, the governance of the sanctuary, the types and appearances of the ex-votos and what would be done with those of most value. The inscriptions tell how the hero spoke to those hoping for his healing ministrations; stelae illustrate the therapy process. The dedication of Archinos, for example (Athens MBN 3369) shows the god standing at the head of a sleeping patient and laying his hands upon him; other members of the divine family, the personifications of healing – the relation of Amphiaraos to Asklepios has clearly been blurred – watch the god in action.

The physical remains of the sanctuary are also extensive, as revealed by excavations on both sides of the ravine which cuts through the site. The temple, altar, spring and other buildings of the cult were situated on the north side of the ravine cut by the Mavrodilessi stream. Across the torrent bed to the south stood dwellings for priests, accommodation for those providing for the pilgrims and for the sick, and, most interesting, a *klepsydra* or water-clock.

Although today's visitor to the site approaches from the west, the ancient pilgrims entered from the east. The patients would come first to some bathing facilities, then arrive at the Long Stoa. This large stoa is over 100 metres long, with a colonnade of about 40 Doric columns along the façade. This served as the *enkoimetêrion*, the place for incubation. Walls built within the interior colonnade created two isolation rooms. There the patients, having sacrificed their rams, wrapped themselves in the fleece and slept on benches placed around the walls of these rooms. Benches along the back wall of the stoa itself provided further places of rest.

Immediately behind and above the Long Stoa stands a small theatre with a circular orchestra. This theatre has been well preserved, especially in the structure of its *skênê*, or stage structure, and partial restoration enhances the understanding of the building. The theatre could have been used, probably was used, for events connected with the games celebrated at the site; in modern times it has been used for drama performances. The filmed version of *Oedipus the King* offered by Films for the Humanities, produced by the Athens Classical Theatre Company with voice-over by James Mason and Claire Bloom, for example, was staged in this theatre. Its location adjacent to the incubation stoa, however, underscores the role it played in the rites associated with the healing cult.

Moving further west the visitor comes upon a series of statue bases, standing in front of a strong retaining wall. In earlier times a less elaborate stoa stood here as the incubation chamber, but as the popularity of cult and cure grew, a larger space was needed and hence the Long Stoa replaced it. The pedestals bear inscriptions which provide information about the people who visited the site and made offerings in thanksgiving. The bronze figures which stood on these have long since vanished, but the names of those who paid for them have remained secure.

Further west the visitor saw the altar of the sanctuary. It was large, one of the largest in antiquity. But, as Pausanias (I.34.3) points out, it was dedicated to several gods, deities identified by engraved plaques attached to each of the altar's several sections. Two names remain: Amphiaraos and Hestia. On the north side of the altar are semi-circular steps, which an inscription labels as the 'theatre of the altar.' Apparently the patients watching the sacrifice sat here. It makes perfect sense: it is far easier for the ill and infirm to sit while watching the smoke of their offerings rise to the god.

Finally the patients would arrive at the temple of the sanctuary. Only the northwest entablature and foundation courses remain, but from ancient descriptions its appearance can be known. The temple of Amphiaraos had a porch of six Doric columns with two semi-columns forming the east ends of the side walls; unlike most Doric temples of Greek design, the temple of Amphiaraos had no encircling colonnade. Also unusual was the bench which ran along the back wall of the *pronaos*, the porch of the temple. If, as has been suggested and seems certain, this bench was for visitors to rest before entering the temple or attending ceremonies, we are given another illustration of how the Amphiareion looked to the particular circumstances of its visitors: they were weak, ill, and found standing for long periods of time difficult.

Inside the temple stood a marble statue of Amphiaraos, while in front of it were set up the *trapezas* or tables on which stood the gold vessels used by the priests for libations and where the most costly ex-votos were displayed. Dozens of other simulacra hung within the temple; some were even fastened onto the statue of the god.

Immediately to the south of the altar runs the sacred spring, described by Pausanias (I.34.4) as the site where 'Amphiaraos rose as a god'. Although the water was considered to be sacred it was not used for bathing or even drinking, but after getting a successful cure, a person was required to throw gold or silver coins into the spring. From these as well as the ex-votos collected and melted the sanctuary received its financial support.

At the end of its active history, the Amphiareion at Oropos differs from other healing sanctuaries. Here no Christian buildings arose over the ancient temples nor was the site ever systematically destroyed. At this site Amphiaraos was the healing divinity, and perhaps this is why no Christian churches were established here: the hero did not pose any threat to Jesus; he was not a rival in the way that Asklepios was. We notice, however, what was not of interest to the Christians, that the same elements that make up Asklepieia for the god are present at the shrine of the hero who heals. While the places for the patients to rest seem to be more numerous at the Amphiareion than at other sanctuaries of Asklepios, temple, altar, and stoas stood here (with one altered in design to be an appropriate sleeping hall). Finally the existence and placement of the theatre shows that it was necessary to have a sacred performance space at any healing sanctuary, be the resident power a god or a hero.

Thus the major healing sanctuaries of the ancient Greek world show common elements. While differences may result from geographic or economic conditions, there are basic structures at all sites: there is always an altar, a temple, a fountain house or other water source, an *abaton*, and a theatre, the latter either within or adjacent to the sanctuary. Each of these spaces played a role in the healing ritual. The patient who came to an Asklepieion took a purifying bath, made offerings at the altar, prayed to the god at the temple, watched a pageant at the theatre, and finally retired to an incubation chamber to dream the cure the god or his servants would bring.

II. Drama and Healing in Ancient Greece

Local Sites

> The sites of Aesculapius' shrines had qualities which all cultures have recognized as ideal for restoring health ... Breeze-touched hills, clear-flowing springs and beautifully cultivated gardens ... [There] sacred serpents anointed injured limbs... and priests intoned magical formulas.
>
> Sherwin B. Nuland, *Doctors: The Biography of Medicine*, 5

In addition to the large, well-known and well-equipped sanctuaries, there were many smaller shrines sacred to the healing god. Scattered in towns around the Greek and Roman world, these offered nearby residents access to the rites and cures of Asklepios. In addition to the standard elements of a sanctuary, a theatre is to be found at or near the majority of these lesser Asklepieia. From the text of Pausanias and archaeological reports we know the layout of many of these sanctuaries.[27] In the following paragraphs I present information about a select few local Asklepieia which have an identified viewing space as part of the sacred site.

Lebena

One of the most famous sanctuaries to Asklepios stood on the south coast of Crete not far from Phaistos. The jutting headland may be the source of its name, as the rocky point there is said to resemble a lion – said to be one of the lions once yoked to the chariot of Rhea. Washed by the Libyan Sea, the complex may first have been a spa around medicinal springs, but by the Hellenistic and Roman periods Lebena was important both as a healing site and as a harbour for the important city of Gortyn. Its patients came from all over Crete and some even journeyed there from Libya.

Overlooking the harbour stood a large temple of Asklepios; in its extant *cella* (central room) an altar and two adjacent columns remain. Its floors were once adorned with alternating marble panels and bright mosaics. Just north of the temple is a building currently identified as the treasury, approached by ascending a monumental staircase.

Immediately adjacent to the staircase archaeologists have found a long *abaton* with a temple to the Nymphs at its east end. *Abaton*, temple, and bathing basins surrounded the medicinal waters. According to Dillon (1994: 248) the *iamata* (inscribed stelae) set up at Lebena seem to be personal, rather than public, i.e. dedicated by individuals rather than set up by the sanctuary personnel as at Epidauros. These record that the patients were healed during their sleep; they do not say they saw the god in their dreams. But they were healed, and people came to the sanctuary in belief that they, too, would leave cured.

There are other structures at Lebena closer to the shoreline. One of these may have been a hotel as it had many small rooms, each with a bay window overlooking the sea. Other buildings seem to have been regular homes for those who worked the harbour or the other facilities of the port.

Lebena seems to lack a theatre, nor has an *odeion* been discovered. But the sanctuary does not lack a public viewing space, for patients could well have sat upon the large steps leading to the treasury, watched a small ritual pageant, then walked the short distance to the *abaton*. As the large stairway is unusual, it may have been designed to provide the requisite viewing area, if the site lacked space or finances for a proper *odeion*. As Lebena was a major local sanctuary of the healing god, it would be odd if its rituals did not include the Asklepieion pageant.

Orchomenos

One of oldest and richest cities of 'heroic Greece', Orchomenos lies some 15 kilometres northeast of Levadhia, near former Lake Kopais. The barren heights of Mt Akontion (Dhourdhouvana) tower behind the city. Traditionally it was said to be the capital of the Minyans, who, according to legend, drained off the Kopaic Lake and built the fortification of Gla. Both the archaeological remains of Orchomenos and the distinctive grey pottery found there prove the existence of a brilliant civilization at the site between the fifteenth and twelfth centuries BC. After suffering periods of destruction at the hands of Thebes during the fourth century, the city was rebuilt by Philip II and Alexander and became a leading city under Macedonian rule. Orchomenos finally fell into decline during the Roman period.

Its most notable archeological remains include a *tholos* tomb and a theatre. In 1886 Schliemann excavated the *tholos*, which he preserved;

the round tomb is distinctive for its side chamber featuring a ceiling adorned with spirals and leaves. A further distinctive element of the *tholos* now stands at its centre: a Macedonian funerary monument, a fine illustration of the *tholos'* continuity as a burial site.

On the east slope of the Akropolis stands the theatre of Orchomenos, built in the late fourth century BC. About 400 metres to the west, a sanctuary of Asklepios has been identified on a second higher terrace; the remains of its Doric temple date from the same period. The placement of the sanctuary may well have been determined by its proximity to the existing theatre, a deciding factor we have seen elsewhere. The entire complex was large and impressive. Two ramparts start from the Asklepieion and climb north and south up the slope to meet at a tower on the summit. Three gates pierce the ramparts. Cross walls run from the edge of the Asklepieion terrace in both directions and serve to define the city.

At the foot of the healing sanctuary lay the sacred spring of the Charites, the Graces, goddesses who were especially venerated at Orchomenos. The Sanctuary of the Charites probably stood where the Convent of the Dormition (Kimisis tis Theotokou) is today; its church was built in AD 874 on the site of the Charites' temple and restored after an earthquake in 1895. As the theatre influenced the placement of the Asklepieion, so here it seems as if the healing power of the pagan deities influenced the building of a Christian sanctuary and once again we see that holy sites remain holy.

While natural geography certainly determined the sanctuary of the Graces at the spring and the theatre on the slope of the Akropolis, the decision to place the Asklepieion in particular relationship and orientation to these must have been deliberate. Here at Orchomenos, as elsewhere, the three elements work together for a single purpose.

Peiraeus/ Mounychia

At Peiraeus, the port of Athens, there were sanctuaries to many deities, and in some cases divinities unique to the area. As a port city Peiraeus had to accommodate the diverse religions of the sailors and merchants coming to the harbour; Corinth, Delos and Ostia, the port of Rome, were similar in offering cult shrines to many different gods. Among the 'standard' deities honoured at Peiraeus was Asklepios.

Although the date of its establishment is not known, the sanctuary of the healing god at Athens' port is well attested, especially if, as some scholars have suggested, the action of Aristophanes' *Ploutos* takes place there. The great theatre of Athens' harbour city was built into the western slope of the area known as Mounychia, while somewhat to the west of the area of Zea a smaller theatre was constructed (and has been recently incorporated into the Peiraeus Archaeological Museum).

The sanctuary of Asklepios was on the promontory east of Zea and at the southwest foot of Mounychia. Thus theatre and sanctuary, while not adjacent, are certainly in the same area of the Peiraeus, that of Mounychia/Zea. Patients, as described by Aristophanes, could bathe in the sea and sleep in the *abaton* of the sanctuary, but it is certainly possible for these same patients to have seen a ritual pageant in the theatre before or after their ritual bathing. Thence they would be ready to retire and await the visitations of the god or his representatives.

Trikka

According to at least one tradition, Asklepios was born at Trikka, and his first sanctuary was established there. Homer says Asklepios' sons came to Troy from Trikka (*Iliad* II.729-33) and Strabo (VIII.360, IX.437) asserts that its Asklepieion is the oldest in Greece. Otherwise its history remains unknown, although the sanctuary seems to have prospered in Roman times. Ancient Trikka lay on the left bank of Lethaios River, but the modern city of Trikala spans both sides, and few remains of the ancient site exist today.

Early excavations at Trikka appear to have discovered the expected Asklepieion and further work in the mid-twentieth century revealed somewhat more of the sanctuary. There seems to have been a large central room with a series of four narrow rooms to the northwest of it, an arrangement that could well be an *abaton*. At some point in the fourth century AD a hypocaust floor was added. A second building stood northwest of the first, while two stoas at right angles to each other adjoined it. The complex, probably dating from the second century BC, appears to be a square surrounded by stoas.

The discovery of fragments of decrees in the courtyard provides the most significant evidence for identifying the structure. Since decrees are frequently placed within a city's chief sanctuary, and Trikka's chief sanctuary must be its Asklepieion, it has been argued that these structures are a part of the Asklepieion. While this identification seems to rest on rather circular evidence and assumptions, the shape of the complex would support the idea that this complex is an Asklepieion. To date, however, no theatre has been discovered at Trikka, and only two of its inscriptions include the name of the healing god. The god's reputed birth site remains the only place in which no theatre has yet been identified as a part of his sanctuary.

Pausanias and Asklepios

Pausanias noted sanctuaries to the healing god in many of the cities he visited. Some were in ruins even in his day, e.g. Naupaktos (X.38.13), while other sites had little more than a simple statue, e.g. Brasiai (III.24.2-5) or Leuktra (III.26.4). On the other hand, many cities had fine temples and images of the healing god that were certainly worth seeing, e.g. an ivory one at Kyllene (VI.26.4-6) and a chryselephantine statue at Sikyon (II.10.2-3).

From time to time Pausanias noted that these sanctuaries were near theatres, although he does not mention that any of them had a viewing space included within the *temenos*. At Megalopolis, for example, a city whose theatre is still worth seeing, he notes that the sanctuary to Asklepios stood adjacent to that theatre. The healing sanctuaries at Aigina and Argos seem to have been near the theatre, a structure still visible at the latter city. Sparta, of course, receives a lengthy discussion in Pausanias' travel book. He identifies two sanctuaries to Asklepios, one near the 'Clubs' above the theatre, housing a special wooden image of the god (III.14.2 and 10), while the finest sanctuary of Asklepios stood at the cattle markets not far from the temple of Aphrodite in Armour. At Phlous Pausanias reports (II.13.5) seeing a shrine to Asklepios on the Akropolis, under which stood a theatre. A large square building with interior colonnades was built adjacent to it; this could be the sanctuary to Demeter that Pausanias says lay not far away, or it could be part of the Asklepieion.[28]

For theatres and Asklepieia beyond Pausanias' texts, I should mention that in her listing of Asklepieia, Semeria (1986) includes Buthrotum (Butrint) in southern Albania, where the theatre and sanctuary of Asklepios are closely associated. Finally I note that at Paphos on Cyprus an *odeion* stands near the sanctuary of the healing god.

At the sanctuaries of Asklepios, whether large or small, regional or local, located in key cities or in remote villages, a theatre (or a viable viewing space) was considered to be an important, indeed essential, structure for the sacred complex. This universal presence of a public viewing space shows that ritual dramas were a part of the dream therapy process and gives a further clue as to why dream therapy worked. Belief and visual prompting brought the deity to the patient's dream.

Athens

One could approach the god of healing either from the west by passing under the keen and watchful gaze of Athena, or from the east by passing through the precinct of rebirth and ecstasy ruled by Dionysos.

Edward Tick, *The Practice of Dream Healing*, 83

The Athenians established a home for Asklepios immediately west of the Theatre of Dionysos on the south slope of the Akropolis. The location is significant. A sanctuary for the god of healing required an accessible spring and space for an *abaton*. On the south slope there was a spring that had long been considered holy; this had been marked off by a wall on which a fifth-century inscription reads *horos krênês*, 'boundary of the fountain' (Wycherley 1978: 181). Inserted here the god's residence could take advantage of a well-defined and well-known spring. While the god now had a source of water, his sanctuary still required extensive construction to accommodate all the necessary elements: access to that spring, a stoa for incubation, and a well-defined sacred boundary, the *temenos*. But the site did have one key ingredient on hand: a fine theatre had already been carved out of the hillside, and so it was not necessary to build a second one. This was a significant factor in the placement of the Asklepieion in Athens.

The god of healing arrived in Athens in the mid-fifth century BC during the celebration of the Eleusinian Mysteries. Two traditions underlie his 'arrival' in the city. One says that when he first came to Athens, he was 'lodged' in the Eleusinion in the southeast section of the Agora, although those who so lodged him are not known, nor do we know in what form: a statue or a snake? The introduction of Asklepios' cult often meant that a sacred snake was brought to the new site and it was assumed the god himself followed shortly after. As the deity had arrived after the start of the annual celebration of the Mysteries, the fourth day of the Eleusinian festival was called the *Epidauria* and was reserved for those who arrived late for the Mysteries. A second tradition links his arrival with the poet Sophocles. A paean (see below) reputedly composed by the tragic poet earned Sophocles the title *Dexion*, as the one who 'welcomed' the deity and gave him accommodation. The poet may have 'welcomed' the god, but, again, in what form is unknown. In noting the playwright's hospitality for the god, Dodds (1951: 193) cites also the remark of Wilamowitz:

> Until a house could be built for [the god], he enjoyed the hospitality of no less a person than the poet Sophocles – a fact which has its bearing on the understanding of Sophocles' poetry. As Wilamowitz observed, one cannot think that either Aeschylus or Euripides would have cared to entertain a Holy Snake.

Sophocles, Dodds implies, would have had no problem in so doing. The belief that it was he who welcomed the deity into his home led to the further belief that the playwright also established the Asklepieion on the south slope of the Akropolis. A paean extant in fragments on the Sarapion monument (*IG* II^2 4510 = Edelstein T-587) is ascribed to Sophocles. It is a prayer to the mother of the god, invoking her to come to the sanctuary:

> O far-famed daughter of Phlegyas, mother of the god who wards off pains ... the unshorn [Phoebus] I begin my loud-voiced hymn
> ...
> accompanied by flutes ... the helper of the sons of Cecrops... may you
> come ... the golden-haired [?] ... him ... the Olympian ...
>
> (tr. Edelsteins)

Sophocles may well have welcomed the cult to Athens or perhaps to Colonus, his birth site, but these lines do not prove he placed the cult on the Akropolis. Other inscriptional evidence has ascertained it was one Telemachos who so placed the god's sanctuary in the location described by Pausanias (I.21.7). Indeed, it seems that when Telemachos first established the sanctuary in Athens in *c.* 420/419 BC it was a private, not a state cult. Just when it became the 'Asklepieion in the City' is uncertain, but it would seem to have been very shortly after Telemachos' introduction of the healing god. For soon it was developed into a proper Asklepieion, with all the elements common to such sites.

After an exhaustive study of the archaeological and inscriptional evidence, Aleshire (1989) asserts that she had determined the limits of the *temenos* by its *peribolos* wall. The city Asklepieion, she writes (34):

Was located on the eastern terrace, between the eastern peribolos of the Pelargikos and the NW arc of the Theatre of Dionysus and fitted in between the Peripatos and the Akropolis rock. [It] consisted originally of a single small temple and the bothros, which functioned as a reservoir or (perhaps less likely) as a sacrificial pit .... At least as early as 300 BC a stoa was constructed to serve as the abaton for the sanctuary; the bothros and the sacred spring were carefully integrated into the plan of this building.

The *propylon* (entry gate) to the sanctuary that is visible today dates from the Roman period. Now only fragments of the ancient stoa remain, scattered pieces of marble dating from the original Greek structure and the later Roman rebuilding of the space once used as the *abaton*. At one time the long stoa had two stories which backed against the wall of the Akropolis with seventeen Doric columns on each floor. In the early years of the twenty-first century, much of this stoa is being restored.

Some hundred metres from the incubation stoa the natural cave of the spring was enlarged, shaped and covered with a domed roof. Just beyond the spring another cutting was made into the rock of the Akropolis. A square raised chamber there held a deep pit, or *bothros*. While no inscriptional evidence identifies the purpose of this pit, it is generally considered to be the home of the sacred serpent that played such an important role in the nightly rituals. A short distance further to the west archaeological excavations have revealed the foundation of a small temple to Asklepios and his daughter Hygieia. A large altar once stood in the centre of the sanctuary. Both temple and altar are also being restored as part of the project to enhance the south slope of the Athenian Akropolis. All requisite elements of the sanctuary were cleverly integrated into the Akropolis slope immediately west of the Theatre of Dionysos.

There is further evidence that the placement of the Asklepieion adjacent to the theatre seems to be deliberate. The festival of Asklepios was officially linked to that of Dionysos. The eighth day of the spring month Elaphebolion was a festival day devoted to Asklepios and considered to be the *proagôn* to the City Dionysia (Aeschines 3.66-7). While Dionysus was honoured with drama and the healing god with hymns, the fact that they shared a day of celebration indicates that the theatre was used in rites honouring both deities. The report by Andocides (*On the Mysteries* 38) indicates that the theatre was used for events other than the performance of drama; other sources suggest the *Boulê* occasionally met there (Mikalson 1975: 123 *et passim*).

Each sanctuary for Asklepios – indeed, every deity's sanctuary – had its resident choristers or *paianistai* who were to sing the paeans on the festival days. At Athens, however, only three lists of *paianistai* have been found and these are all connected with the cult of the healing god (Aleshire 1991: 38). As suggested earlier, at those sites sacred to the healing god the tasks of the *paianistai* included taking part in the pageants enacted for the patients before they retired to the *abaton* for the night. Among the many dedicants whose names are known from the Athenian Asklepieion, there seem to have been several who may well have been among those who took part in the ritual pageants. From Aleshire's exhaustive prosopographic register of all who made dedications to the god of healing I include here those who are identified as actors. While it is certainly possible that these were professional players in the annual dramas presented at the City Dionysia who happened to have been cured by the god, it is more likely that these men were recognized at the Asklepieion for their participation in the ritual pageants.

The 29 names listed on one side of the Sarapion Monument perhaps form a complete choir.[29] As most of these men were citizens of Athens or had citizen rights, this is not a listing of those who came as or with envoys sent to the city, but of those residents who stepped forward to participate in honouring the god. These names seem to indicate a choir, but individuals can be singled out (Aleshire 1991: 98, 110). One Titos Phlabios Glaukias Glaukiou Acharneus was an actor for whom an honorary statue was erected at the Asklepieion. Surely he must have been so honoured because of the role(s) he played in the pageant for Asklepios; it would make no sense for a professional actor of the Dionysian stage to have his statue put up in the sanctuary of the healing god. His brother, Titos Diophantos Glaukiou Acharneus, also received an honorary statue, which seems to indicate that this was a family of actors performing in the service of Asklepios.

While the family names of other individual *paianistai* included in the register are known, these men are not known as actors and thus their role in the pageants is not evident. At least one *hierophylax* (keeper of the temple) is also named, Eukarpos Dionysiou Phalereus, and several dedicants, some of whom were physicians, some well-known scholars, are among those whose names have survived in the Asklepieion inscriptions. But it is through the names of those who sang and acted for the god that we can imagine what transpired as evening fell on the Athenian Asklepieion. The patients sat expectantly in the Theatre of Dionysos and watched a torch-lit pageant in which the healing god laid his hands upon a suffering figure, an individual who soon arose and rejoiced to be finally cured.

The Athenian state contributed to the support of the cults practised within its boundaries through various systems of taxation, and an extant tax document indicates a payment of one drachma 'for Asklepios.' The initiation of a tax for the divine healer is easily explained. As Asklepios was a late introduction into the Athenian roster of deities, his cult would have lacked a long-established source of revenue. Thus the city created a tax to cover this lack (Schlaifer 1940: 240). Although it is not possible to know for certain on whom the tax was levied, it can be assumed it was a general taxation paid by all for the public good. Some have suggested that the drachma was 'the Athenian version of the *iatrikon*'. This was a tax levied on all citizens to pay the public physicians, what we might perhaps consider a sort of ancient health insurance. 'It is not impossible,' writes Schlaifer (1940: 241), 'that their official headquarters were his temple, and that the tax levied for their pay was called "the drachma of Asclepius".' The physicians were closely connected with Asklepios and made a collective offering to the god two times a year, perhaps on their own behalf and on behalf of the patients they had cured (Gorrini 2005: 144-5; cf. *IG* II^2 772 N12). Furthermore, comparison with other cities who levied an *iatrikon* suggests that this was a general tax, not one paid by the sick. Perhaps the benefits of having a sanctuary to Asklepios in the city outweighed the usual Athenian aversion to direct taxation. A 'drachma for Asklepios' might seem a small price to pay for the privilege – and honour – of having a healing sanctuary easily available on the south slope of the Akropolis.

Athens' Asklepieion, as would be expected, attracted many visitors. Numerous votive offerings (*anathêmata*) and inscriptions attest to the cures the god provided there. Many patients dedicated the standard terracotta representations of the body part healed, but many others offered richer tokens – silver vases, gold ornaments and coinage. During the *kathairesis*, the annual collection process, the priests removed the gold and silver ex-votos to be melted down and made into new cult equipment. Many of the finer pieces, and certainly the coins were removed and deposited in the state treasury in the back room of the Parthenon.

Most of the visitors to the sanctuary on the Akropolis were Athenians or from near Athens; indeed Wells (1998: 41) asserts, 'It is at once obvious that the Asklepieion at Athens was patronized by families.' Inscriptions and votive stelae showing family groups in supplication to the god underscore these observations. The patients at Athens suffered from ailments similar to those experienced by people elsewhere; the main difference is that from time to time the Athenians seemed to have had more eye trouble than other illnesses, for eye dedications outnumber those of other body parts. In the modern world one could speculate that the Athenian sanctuary 'specialized' in eye cures,[30] but as the god treated all parts of the body, not only ailing eyes, there must be other reasons for the prevalence of eye problems. As Hippokrates makes special reference to the seasonal aspects of illness, perhaps the winds in the mid-250s BC were especially dust-laden in the spring.

Although Telemachos was the one responsible for bringing the god to Athens, Asklepios' cult and his sanctuary very soon came under state control; his 'lodging' in the Eleusinian in the Agora was brief. Athens was eager to establish a regular sanctuary for this important deity, for the city needed the healing god, and an appropriate site for his temple was available. The fact that it was fitted in among the numerous existing cult sites on the south slope of the Akropolis shows the city had a genuine interest in having an Asklepieion within its boundaries and wished to include it in an area where so many of its important sanctuaries were located.

III

Drama and Healing in the Contemporary American Hospital

Case Study: Shands Hospital at the University of Florida

A hospital is only a building until you hear the slate hoofs of dreams galloping upon its roof. You listen then and know that here is no mere pile of stone and precisely cut timber but an inner space full of pain and relief.

Richard Selzer, *Taking the World in for Repair*, 238

[Playback] is an art that is committed to affirming ordinary people's experience and to fostering connections between them so that the communities we live in can grow in compassion and humanity. We strive to hone our art in order to offer it as service.

Jo Salas, 'What is "Good" Playback Theatre?', in Fox and Dauber, *Gathering Voices*, 22

The Arts-in-Medicine (A.I.M.) program at Shands Hospital was created and established by Drs John Graham-Pole and Mary Rockwell Lane in 1991. They envisioned and then began a program that brought together artists who create in various media – music, painting, dance and writing. Some years later, theatre was added to the arts program. All of these media touch the patients and lift their feelings, whether they are witnesses to the art or participate in its creation. According to Graham-Pole and Lane (1994: 19) the directors and the artists make a 'clear distinction between art that patients, clients, or other subjects passively enjoy ... and art that participants create themselves'. The latter is more effective in the healing process of illness, both physical and psychological, because the more involved the patients are in the creative expression, the more they are able, in Graham-Pole's words, 'to take charge of their situation'. While all the artists report the joy

81

their interaction with patients gives both parties, this book focuses on the role of drama in the Arts-in-Medicine program. I write this chapter in the first person, as I have been acting at the Hospital since 2001.

The form of drama we use is Playback Theatre. Jonathan Fox created Playback Theatre in 1974. Fox was inspired by early oral narrative such as that of Homer and believed it could be vital once again. Thus he developed a form of theatre, a non-scripted improvisational form of theatre that is an oral composition, but without the verbal formulas of Homeric epic.[1] In this type of theatre, actors learn a framework through which they can dramatize the story. This framework consists of distinct forms which the troupe uses to *play back* a story's action; the forms function for the Playback actors as do the formulas of oral composition for the epic bard. A Playback performance offers an entirely improvised non-scripted drama.

At a Playback performance, the troupe leader gleans from an audience member a story, a narrative heard by the leader, the players and the audience. When the story has been told, the troupe leader suggests a form to the actors, who then play back the essence of that story to the teller and the other members of the audience. The actors who perform in Playback have a greater interest in their audience than in their own stage presence: it is the outcome of the performance, not its polish or theatrical effect that matters.

Playback Theatre is most commonly practised in the public arena, enacted as a community experience. It was used extensively, for example, in New York City and elsewhere after 9/11/2001. It is also used in educational settings and occasionally when a social statement needs to be made. From the concept of theatre as developed by Jonathan Fox and the workshops offered by Fox and his co-director, Jo Salas, regional groups have taken Playback Theatre around the world, first to Australia, then to the Scandinavian countries, and it is now performed in most of Europe and in Israel.

Before turning to a discussion of how we use Playback Theatre in a hospital setting, it is important to distinguish between Playback Theatre, Psychodrama, and Drama Therapy. The use of drama in healing has been extensively studied and practised during the last thirty years. The belief that cures could come through enactment has attracted psychologists and people in theatre in both America and England. Their study frequently includes anthropological work, for in cultures more closely tied to shamanism and ritual, drama has long played a role as part of the healing process.

Dramatherapy (one word, coined by Peter Slade, for England) and Drama Therapy (two words, as used in America) focus on the patient in need of psychological assistance. Some practitioners have also included the socially dispossessed within their use of drama as therapy. Psychodrama and drama therapy are not identical, but are similar in that both use the patients as the actors; it is the patients who must come to realize their situation through an enactment.

Leaders in the field include, among many others, Sue Jennings in England, J.L. Moreno in Europe and America, and Robert Landy in America. Moreno – although he focused on the therapeutic effects for patients who 'acted out' their issues – also asserted that there is benefit for all who participate in a psychodrama, the audience and the director as well as the patient. This unity creates a sense of community even while the focus is upon the individual. From this discovery, Moreno also created sociodrama, wherein members of a group identify a problem and act out possible solutions.[2]

Drama therapy is a recognized curriculum in England and has a national organization in the United States. Those who do psychodrama are specially trained in psychology if not in drama. The practitioners of drama therapy have training in both theatre and psychology. Their work is used exclusively in a therapeutic context: those who participate are in need of a cure. The vast amount of literature on drama therapy and psychodrama focuses upon the catharsis experienced by the patient when he/she comes to terms with a psychological situation.

The world of the hospital and that of the theatre complement each other, according to Homan (1994), for each is starkly real: real men and women act out significant moments in life and death. Reality and fiction blur on the stage, however, while in the hospital only reality is present. Homan works mainly to make the reality of illness more bearable for those trapped within it. By creating fictions for them to act out, he opens them up to a world beyond their suffering and pain. Improvisational theatre allows patients, especially young patients, to direct their energy to something positive, even if it is an enactment of their unhealthy situation. The excitement of doing and creating does more to lift the spirit than drugs or the kindest of ministrations.

Homan also conducts drama workshops for physicians, asking them, for example, to act out how they will tell a patient unexpectedly bad news. In this way, he argues, they can view their actions before they are completed; the rehearsal will help the doctor more sympathetically connect with the terminally ill patients and their families. More extensive communication training through drama is carried out by Dr Susan Massad of Long Island College Hospital in Brooklyn. Calling her program 'Performance of Doctoring' (POD), Dr Massad works with professional actors to set up improvised theatre games to teach doctors how to communicate more effectively with their patients. Doctors and 'patients', she writes, create scenes in which:

> They use the language of improvisation, especially the 'offer' – a performer's statement, gesture, or even silence, to which another performer responds. The responses, in turn, become new offers through which the performers collaboratively create and build the performance. The program is based on social therapy, a 'performatory' approach to psychotherapy, meaning that it focuses on continuous growth and development, rather than diagnosing and solving problems. The goal is to help doctors use their scientific knowledge of medicine while responding to patients' subjective experience of illness, both factors in 'producing health'.[3]

In his study, *Catharsis in Healing, Ritual, and Drama*, Scheff (1979) follows similar lines. He writes that in cathartic drama (that which is neither too Apolline, i.e. too devoted to thought, nor too Dionysian, too devoted to emotion), the audience can share the emotions of the actors, allowing them to identify with the performers' group. 'In dramas of the cathartic type,' he writes (157), 'with the audience being included in a shared awareness with one or more of the characters, ... the effect is subtle but powerful.' Dramatic scenes move an audience because they touch upon repressed emotions. They need not be exactly equivalent to an individual's experience; certain events are universal. To create scenes which give the most opportunity for discharging distressful emotion, Scheff writes (163), the scene must touch upon repressed emotions that are shared by most members of the audience and are so constructed that the audience is involved, but not overwhelmed.

III. Drama and Healing in the Contemporary American Hospital

Playback Theatre, on the other hand, takes a different approach. Fox came to the idea of Playback through a desire to recreate the context of the Homeric tales. As Simon (1978: 79) has pointed out in his discussion of epic as therapy, participation with an audience can bring a sense of consolation. He asserts (79), 'The shared experience of listening to a tale that expresses the group's fundamental values, beliefs, and aspirations serves to restore us to and reintegrate us with that group.' In Playback Theatre as created by Fox, drama is used to retell an individual's story. The teller becomes audience of his/her own story, and the others who listen share that experience. The link here is between narrative and drama, oral performance doubly told: first by the individual, then by the actors. The stories are enacted in an atmosphere of respect, empathy is a major goal, and the healing comes in the sense of community that is generated when an individual's story is shared with others.

The use of Playback Theatre in the hospital setting as practised at Shands Hospital at the University of Florida is unique. Paula Patterson introduced the idea, bringing the art of this non-scripted theatre to the hospital's public areas and then to a patient's bedside.[4] The idea of Playback Theatre, that the audience is the centre of attention, is special in the hospital setting. There the patients tell their stories, and the narrative is given dramatic form by the acting troupe. While the actual enactment is no different from that done in a community performance, the atmosphere is more highly charged when the teller is a patient. The emotional context is deeply moving for both audience and actors. The patients see their story, their suffering, in a new way. The actors who participate in the A.I.M. Playback Theatre report that they also benefit from the experience, that the improvised performances they give for the patients are more fulfilling than those they do in a regular theatre. It has been noted that one power of art is that it gives the creator a gift and 'the healing power of love',[5] a statement with which the members of the Shands drama troupe can agree. As Simon (1978: 87) pointed out (in discussing the bard and his audience, the bard *qua* therapist), 'The bard is a participant with his patient in a process of healing that exploits a rhythm of dedifferentiation and reintegration of the individual.' If we replace 'bard' with 'Playback actor' the statement rings true for the performances given by A.I.M. in the hospital setting.[6]

In the *pathography*[7] of his journey through cancer, Frank (1991/2002) writes about a patient's need, in this book his own need, to talk about what was happening during the course of an illness, for illness is the experience of living through the disease (13). He descries the typical physician who separates the body from the person. He writes (8-10), 'Doing *with* the body is only part of what needs to be done *for* the person; no one should be asked to detach his mind from his body and then talk about the body as a thing, out there.' He continues (14), 'You cannot be told that you have had a heart attack without having a great deal to express and needing to express it. The problem is finding someone who will help you work out the terms of that expression.' Playback Theatre offers the opportunity to do that.

In the process as used by *Reflections*, the drama troupe at Shands Hospital, the patients relate a problem, a story, a significant event of their life, or a dream they have for their future when they are healed. Once a patient has told a story, the troupe leader (immediately) determines which form will be used, and the actors (immediately) create a set of scenes, sentences, or songs that capture the essence of the patient's words. The actors express the pain, if that has been told, but also suggest a healing. The improvisation is guided by a series of dramatic forms, and these forms or techniques may be briefly described. In 'Story Tableaux', a series of three snap-action tableaux are formed to illustrate the story's theme. The Director gives a single sentence expressing each part of the story's idea and the cast members form a unified tableau of that idea. In 'Fluid Sculpture', a mini dance or swirling motion tells the key points of the patient's story. In 'Sound Sculpture', a line of actors, hands joined, run a series of thoughts illustrating the story's theme up and down the line, with the climax at the turning point of the line. The ideas are often expressed in song as well as words. 'Action Haiku' is a form in which two actors work together, one speaking, one moulding, to create a brief expression of a theme. 'Pairs' (or 'Mixed Feelings') presents the conflicts within the patient's mind; the actors, moving as two stems of a single plant, express the positive and the negative emotions the patient is experiencing, his/her fear and expectation, despair and hope. In 'String of Pearls', the first and last ideas of a story are expressed, then other members of the troupe add sentences as pearls; when all sentences are strung together, the story has been told as a string of pearls. In the most developed form of Playback Theatre, an entire story is enacted. The story must have three parts, beginning, middle and end, with each act highlighting one aspect of the teller's story.

The theory behind Playback Theatre when done in a hospital setting follows the three-fold approach outlined by Jo Salas (1996[2]: 111-12).[8] First, patients need to tell their stories at a time when identity itself has been compromised. As Risse (1999: 9) puts it, '[Patient] stories provide valuable insights into the universe of meanings and emotions surrounding patienthood.' The patient is so often reduced to an identity that seems fully defined by the plastic i.d. bracelet and the chart which labels the bed's occupant as 'a hernia', a 'type-2 melanoma', or 'the lymphoma in bed 651B'. Medicine acts on and with the body, but it seldom addresses the person receiving that medicine. We know, however, that Descartes' dualism is not valid, that mind and body work together, in sickness as well as in health. As Frank (2002:10) writes: 'My body is the means and medium of my life; I live not only in my body but also through it.' The mind is never detached from the body, nor the body from the soul.

Second, the patients tell their stories in an atmosphere of respect, again an atmosphere frequently lacking in a hospital. It is difficult to believe that the nurse or especially the doctor can truly respect the person garbed in the infamous back-opened gown and lying abed with various tubes bringing various things into and out of the body. Third and most important is the aesthetic element of the process, a process that distils life into art. When an individual's experiences are reflected in aesthetic form, new meaning is given to that experience. Here the emotional context is deeply moving. Through a Playback performance the patients see their situation in a new way. It has become something separate, yet personal; the medical experience is given its own identity when transformed into a small moment of art.

A sense of reassurance arises from that newly created meaning. And that reassurance becomes an important ingredient in the healing process. Seeing their story performed helps the patients to come to terms with it; personal distress is alleviated by the players' re-enactment. Frank noted (4) that, 'Talking back is how we find our own experiences in a story someone else has written.' The Playback pieces are not written, but the enactment helps patients see their own experiences in a new way; the communal setting allows them to see that others share the same pain and fear they do. 'Expression,' as Frank has written (34), 'implies the presence of others, and we begin again to share in humanity.' The patient whose story is told in the presence of others shares the experience of those who listened to the ancient bard and saw their cultural values re-enforced and validated. In seeing their story performed, the patients can come to terms with it; the personal issue becomes generalized by the players' re-enactment; the scene takes the suffering away from the patient, alleviates it by elevating it to a more impersonal level. Even when a patient's story is performed bedside, the effect on the patient is immediately noticeable. Scheff's advice (quoted above) is important for Playback Theatre done in the hospital setting, both in theory and as the *Reflections'* own troupe experience has shown.

Every week the actions of *Reflections* are validated by their interaction with the patients, either bedside or in a common space. The Arts-in-Medicine program at Shands recognizes that doctors cannot play the only role in their patients' lives; medicine seeks a cure for disease but it does not enter into the experience of that disease. Our drama troupe seeks to play a role in the patients' healing process. We do not address disease, but we do address illness. The patients experience the disease but they suffer the illness. As Stein (2007: 112) has written, 'Illness is a matter of critical moments, of long and peculiar and memorable days.' Through our listening, distilling and re-enacting, we seek to offer a different approach to the patients' condition, to assist them in facing those long, peculiar and memorable days.[9]

*

Although I am now a member of the drama troupe, my first experience with the process came when I attended a performance by *Reflections* in the B.M.T.U. (Bone Marrow Transplant Unit) as an observer. I was amazed at how much happiness was generated in a room where people were facing very serious illness and their attendant family members shared their suffering. One patient was clearly having a very bad day, and her dream was so simple: to be healed and away. The group did her story in a 'Sound Sculpture' that managed to offer hope and brought an evident sense of peace to this woman in her pain. The patients were startled at how clearly the actors expressed the emotions they were feeling and the events they had told about. When the patients left, there was absolutely no doubt but that at least one long day of their hospital stay had been brightened. Each patient seemed to have already a positive outlook – these would be the survivors – and the actors by their talent and their caring had brought a ray of hope to these people, these patients who came to watch masked and plugged into their medical machines. One patient, upon leaving the hospital after his course of therapy, stated that he believed that the drama had done as much for his healing as had the care of the doctors and the medicines he received.

Reflections most often performs in the public lounge on the heart-transplant floor. Ambulatory patients come together to tell their stories, see them enacted, and share their common emotions. One day a patient, who had suffered a stroke and was now awaiting a heart transplant, came to the lounge angry about his lot, about his handicapped and now limited life. Our 'String of Pearls' version of his story recognized his frustration and pain, but also looked to the new life a new heart would bring. He was visibly moved and visibly encouraged. That same day a woman whose operation had gone wrong and forced her return to the hospital attended the 'show'. She was in despair: who would tend her seven fatherless children if she did not get well? How would she cope? She had no family to visit her. The actors offered her a 'River' of compassion and hope; later they also brought her art and journal supplies. Her tears finally dried and she left the lounge with a smile, escorted by those who had shown her that someone honoured her and cared for her pain.

On other occasions our drama troupe takes the performance bedside. There, too, the magic works. For example, one patient we visited was just at the end of his long journey through dialysis and had received a kidney transplant. We asked him about his dreams for his new life. He had always wanted to drive trucks. We did a 'Sound Sculpture', envisioning his journey, seeing it just over the horizon, for he was alive now with the gift God had given him. With tears rolling down his cheeks he exclaimed, 'That's it! I can see it! I can taste it! I can feel it! You have put before me my life rolling out ahead of me.' His parents were there and the emotion shared in that room in those moments was tangible; we were all united in the patient's dream for his healthy life.[10]

Once we visited bedside a man who was awaiting heart surgery. He welcomed us in, but did not really want to share much information, giving but monosyllabic answers; he was scared but unwilling to admit it; he probably was in pain. From the few hints he did give us – he had, despite his hesitancy in telling us, had an interesting life – we retold in two forms two parts of his story: first of his days as cook on a submarine, then of his adventures as a postman. As we finished, he was laughing and was sharing more details of his life; as we left he thanked us warmly for our visit. For a while, at least, his spirits were brighter and he was ready to face the next day in a more optimistic mood.

On another occasion we entered the room of an elderly woman. But when we tried to talk with her she barely responded. The weight of her illness was too great. Two of us wondered if we should just say goodbye, but our third said to give it a try. So we did the familiar 'Pairs', in which two actors reflect the mixed emotions of the teller – and in the hospital the patients always have mixed feelings. We did little more than our almost standard 'I am suffering here in the hospital' but 'I know that I am in God's hands'. The patient sat up, tears streamed down her face, she embraced us, thanked us for expressing exactly what she was feeling. We left quietly; we knew that we had touched her in a way that no one in the medical profession had done.

On another day of bedside theatre, we played to a woman whose strength of character was evident even during her time of sickness. Her daughters, all successful women, were gathered together in her room. We did a simple 'Alphabet Game', a form in which each sentence of the scene begins with the next letter of the alphabet. Our story told about the family interaction, how this matriarch had guided and shaped the lives of her daughters. Somehow we found the right words to describe her and her family; there was not a dry eye in the room: 'You hit it perfectly!' the women exclaimed. When by chance one daughter, in charge of the hospital recovery room, saw me there many months later, she still remembered the memories we had evoked that day we played theatre in her mother's room.

Sometimes it seems that the intensity in the air of the hospital room is touched by magic, as troupe members connect with the patient by adding details never expressed. Some time ago three of us went bedside to visit a dear friend of mine. She had elected to give up her multi-year battle against cancer; I knew she would be leaving us soon. But her spirits that day were bright and she was looking forward to seeing what she had heard about. We decided upon 'Orlando Monologue' as our method; in this form a simple object is described individually by three members of the troupe. On this day we used a pair of her slippers as our prop. I knew Karla well, so my monologue was based on places and parts of her life that were factual and cloaked in memories. Our second speaker took a lighter tone and brought a smile to Karla's face. The third actress took the slipper. She made it into an heirloom, one in which Karla might have tucked a coin from her Bavarian grandmother. 'Yes!' Karla exclaimed. 'My grandmother was from Bavaria!' I had known this woman for thirty years but did not know that; our third actress had met her ten minutes before.

Reflections offers bedside and community room theatre every Thursday afternoon. The troupe's own memories are full of the times when a performance brought an emotional catharsis, a moment of tears, or a smile of joy to the patient or patients who witnessed their stories retold through the medium of Playback Theatre. The magic of drama played a role in uplifting the patients' spirits, thus assisting in the interaction between body and mind that contemporary medicine recognizes as vital to the healing process.

When I first learned about the therapeutic benefits of arts in medicine I was both intrigued and sceptical: an interesting idea, but could it work? Personal observation and participation, however, have changed my mind. The patients, who have terrible illnesses and must wait so long for their hoped-for operations, are wonderfully receptive to the sort of emotional catharsis which the drama troupe brings. Equally positive results arise from art, music or dance performances; art seems to be particularly effective when the patients' own creative abilities direct their attention away from their immediate suffering. But drama, in which verbal and physical expression is given to the patients' dreams and fears, does more than distract: it offers a larger view and opens up a realm of possibilities.

As a scholar and student of drama, I found this means of bringing hope to a patient intriguing in another way. Playback Theatre in the hospital setting seemed a reversal of the usual response to a theatrical performance, where we (a healthy audience) empathize with the experience of the characters and make the general more personal. In the hospital setting, the personal is, through the drama performance, made more universal. Through the enactment of drama, for both hospital patient and theatre audience, the catharsis Aristotle described occurs and leads to a healthier soul.

Asklepios Beyond the Classical World

I swear by Apollo physician, and Asklepios, and Hygieia and
Panakeia and all the gods and goddesses ...

> Hippokrates, *Hippokratic Oath*, 1

1. Asklepios and Jesus

While the frequency of a church or chapel built within or adjacent to
the ruined temples of many ancient deities is notable worldwide – holy
sites remain holy – we find a special continuity at the former sanctuaries of Asklepios. At many of the sites once dedicated to the healing
god, close by or atop his temples there are now churches dedicated to
Saints Kosmas and Damian. Their icons are reputed to have healing
qualities, and within the church the iconostasis is hung with
anathêmata showing the various body parts that have been healed. In
many instances, however, the new churches have been constructed
over an Asklepieion that seems to have been deliberately destroyed.
The Christians who moved into the ancient sanctuaries apparently
had more than a desire to take advantage of a site already holy; they
wanted to purge the area of its earlier inhabitants.

Why did the followers of Christ feel it so necessary to build over the
temples to the healing god, to stamp out and obliterate the cult of
Asklepios? It has been frequently noted that Asklepios was the Greek
divinity that most challenged Jesus, for followers of the ancient god
saw little difference between the accomplishments of their long-re-
vered healing deity and those of Jesus of Nazareth. He seemed to be
the pagan god most feared by the new Christians, for while the other
ancient deities could be discounted, the many close parallels between
Asklepios and Jesus made him a particular threat to the early Christian teachers.

Both entered the world in miraculous birth: sired by a god, they
were born from mortal mothers. Their births were celebrated with a

93

divine light: a lightning flash drove the curious shepherd from the baby Asklepios, and shining angels announced Jesus' birth to the shepherds watching their flocks and a bright star guided men to his cradle. Both could heal beyond what might be expected, both could raise men from the dead. Both had a holy father and acted as agents of that father: Asklepios took over Apollo's role as healing god, Jesus came to earth in the name of God. Most importantly, both healed miraculously and both could even raise men from the dead, although Asklepios was punished for doing this and Jesus apparently tried it only once. The morality of both was impeccable; Asklepios, unlike so many other Greek divinities, was always faithful to his wife Epione, while Jesus apparently eschewed all sexual alliances. I note in passing that even art reflects the similarity: both Asklepios and Jesus are represented as kindly in appearance, youthful – but bearded; statues of the Greek god and frescoes of the Christian deity present them as accessible to their followers.[1]

Furthermore, the god of healing had concern even for those whom he could not cure. He felt sympathy for mortals – a quality mostly lacking in true (full) Greek divinities. His association with the Eleusinian Mysteries has already been noted – in both cults the ritual pageant was important – but a further association might be that both Asklepios and the goddesses of Eleusis look to what happens after death. It has been suggested that many believed that the moment of death was the moment of initiation into a new life, one into which Asklepios would escort them; some say that Socrates' final enigmatic words, 'We owe a cock to Asklepios', show his belief that the healing god would lead him to the next life.[2] Certainly Jesus was concerned about the afterlife of mortals; he could not save the lives of all people who came to him but he could save their souls.

In noting the similarities between Asklepios and Jesus, it is important to note also how the god of healing differed from other gods of the Greek pantheon. Asklepios, unlike Apollo, did not cause disease nor use it as a punishment. A further and important distinction is set out perceptively and persuasively by Garland (1992) 134:

A feature of the worship of Asklepios which sharply distinguished it from conventional Greek religion is that it was concerned with the needs of the individual rather than those of the state ... Of all the gods, it was Asklepios who came closest to challenging the polytheistic basis of Greek religion and who in consequence was destined to pose the most serious challenge to Christianity.

There were differences between Asklepios and Jesus: the Greek god had a regular family who attended and assisted him, Jesus had followers but during his lifetime they had no miraculous powers of their own. Believers in Asklepios considered him but one of many; faith in Jesus demanded the denial of all other gods. And most significant, of course: Asklepios returned from the realm of the dead and remained on earth; Jesus rose from the dead, ascended to heaven and has not returned.

Furthermore, faith in Jesus was itself a power for healing. His touch, even the touch of his garment, was believed to heal. While Asklepios also laid his hands upon his patients, he did so while they were asleep in his *abaton*; his cures were tied to his sanctuaries. There were several hundred Asklepieia as we have seen, but patients had to go to them; Asklepios did no marketplace healing. Asklepios and Jesus also differed in what they expected or demanded of the sick. The Greek god was content with small offerings (a cock, a cup) and a thankful inscription; Jesus required that those who sought his cure believed in him and all he stood for. Temkin (1991: 97) points out a further and important difference between the Greek and Christian deities: 'Altogether there exists an essential difference between Asklepios and Jesus: the Greek god cured because this was his function, whereas Jesus healed in fulfilment of a divine mission.'[3] Another difference between the two lay in the method of cure: the Greek god was first of all a physician; he acted as a doctor and his cures frequently came from such methods and drugs (*pharmaka)* as a doctor might prescribe, whereas Jesus cured by a touch or word those who came to him in belief. Finally and most significantly, Asklepios cured the diseases of mortal bodies; Jesus claimed to cure both body and soul.

However it was because of his care and concern for human suffering that in time Asklepios became the greatest challenger to Jesus and his teaching. Justin, writing in the second century AD, perhaps most directly equates the two (*Apologia* 22.6 = Edelstein T-94):

When we say he [Jesus] made well the lame ... and resurrected the dead, we shall seem to be mentioning deeds similar to and even identical to those said to have been done by Asklepios.

Justin also describes the death and resurrection of Christ as 'nothing new and different ... [from that of Asklepios] who, although being a great healer, having been struck by thunder went up into heaven' (*Apologia* 21.1-2 = Edelstein T-335).

An injunction to purity was inscribed above the door of the temple to Asklepios at Epidauros (Edelstein T-336): 'Pure must be the one who enters the fragrant temple, Purity is to think holy thoughts.' When Clement of Alexandria, writing in the late second century AD, quotes the inscription in a passage teaching Christian virtues, he sets the stage for those who would wish to destroy the pagan temple, for such a linking would easily arouse a desire to eradicate any evidence which would enhance or continue belief in the earlier deity of healing. At the Greek god's most important sanctuary, the desire was carried out. Tomlinson (1983: 33) notes that the destruction of Epidauros was clearly deliberate.

While Asklepios presented the greatest challenge to Jesus and his religion, the Greek belief in the pagan gods and especially in the teaching of the philosophers was not laid aside at the first Christian edict against them. As Alison Frantz has argued (1975), the Athenians reconstructed the house of Plutarch for the Head of the Neoplatonic Academy on the south slope of the Akropolis, adjacent to the restored (if altered) Theatre of Dionysos. She quotes (31) Proklos' biographer that the Head of the Academy 'enjoyed his house because of its proximity to the temple and theatre of Dionysos and to the temple of Asklepios'. After the Herulian devastation in AD 267 the Athenians built over the ruins a huge complex now identified as the ancient University of Athens. Frantz says (34) the familiar Giants of the Agora stood before this new pagan school, and that the statues were not merely convenient decoration. For they not only survived 'purification by fire', i.e. consignment to the lime kiln, but they were not branded in the usual way with a cross to stop their anti-Christian power.

2. Healing Saints of the Greek Orthodox Church

We act in faith, and miracles occur.

Dag Hammarskjöld, *Markings*, 17

In other locations, however, assimilation rather than destruction guided belief in the new healer God. The saints that took over the realm of Asklepios for the Greek and Catholic Churches are Saints Kosmas and Damian, and in Athens and Peiraeus, for example, their church arose on the foundations of Asklepios' temples. Kosmas and Damian, who lived during the late 200s AD, were twins, elders of three younger brothers, who had learned the arts of medicine at an early age. After practising their healing skills at the seaport of Aegea, they went to the Roman province of Syria. They became well known on two accounts: they took no payment for their work and they had exceptional medical ability. The first action earned them the name *anargyroi*, or 'silverless ones', which later Christian writers attributed to their exact following of Jesus' words: 'Cure the sick, raise the dead, cleanse those suffering from leprosy, drive out devils. You received without charge, give without charge' (Matthew 10:8). The second was enhanced after they replaced a leg amputated for ulcers by grafting a leg from a recently dead man in its place.

In performing this miraculous surgery, the saints' method echoes an incubation miracle at a sanctuary of Asklepios. After telling the amputee to go into the house of god and pray, Kosmas and Damian got the leg of a dead man and attached it to the sleeping patient. Upon awaking, the patient claimed to have witnessed the operation in a dream while the saints declared they had been directed in their action by a dream.

Despite their following, their practised vows of poverty and their medical skills, the brothers ran foul of the Roman government. Christianity was not tolerated in the Roman Empire until the days of Constantine (AD 330s) and the Roman emperor Diocletian (AD 284-305) was especially hostile to the newly spreading cult. Thus under his persecution, Kosmas and Damian were arrested by an otherwise unknown prefect, Lysias, who tortured them to recant. They refused to deny their faith – according to some accounts the tortures did them

97

no harm – and finally the Roman ruler ordered them to be beheaded. Thus in 303 they met their death – some thirty years before they might have practised in peace. Their younger brothers joined them in their martyrdom and many paintings show all five laid out in a single grave.

As Kosmas and Damian were now considered to be martyrs, soon many churches and other religious buildings were dedicated to them and pieces of their bodies became revered relics.[4] They were originally buried in Cyrus in Syria and Justinian dedicated the city in their honour. However, he brought their bodies to Constantinople and interred them there, although several churches around the world claim skulls and other parts of their bodies,[5] and soon the very dust from their graves was believed to have healing power.

Although Christian leaders insisted on the difference between Asklepios and the saints, some fundamental similarities remained. For example, the followers of Christianity found that secular and religious healing did not deny each other, even as the choice between sanctuary and the local *iatros* were not mutually exclusive for the ancient Greeks. The healing god and the healing saints also shared characteristics: as Asklepios had been a mortal skilled in medicine before becoming a god, so Kosmas and Damian were physicians before they became saints. They had used drugs and surgical skills during their lifetime; it was only after their death that merely touching their remains healed the believer.

As sanctuaries for Asklepios had been created around the world, so churches dedicated to Kosmas and Damian were built in numerous cities; frequently these churches arose adjacent to, or even upon, an ancient Asklepieion. As an ancient Greek might put up a monument or temple to Asklepios in thanksgiving, so in Constantinople, Justinian, after he himself was cured of an illness, built a church dedicated to them. Furthermore, as Risse (1999: 72) points out, when the first hospital was built in that city, a small chapel to Kosmas and Damian was put up adjacent to it.[6] In Corinth, silvery images of body parts are hung in the chapel of Saints Kosmas and Damian that stands just beyond the ancient Asklepieion. In Athens a basilica to the two was constructed adjacent to the god's sanctuary, and now fragments of the Christian church and Asklepios' sanctuary lie intermingled on the south slope of the Acropolis. *Anathêmata* were hung in all these churches to Kosmas and Damian. The healing saints took up the arts of Asklepios and took over the places of his worship, while the offerings made by those who have been cured keep the dedicatory acts of the ancient Greeks alive.

V

Conclusion and Epilogue

> Context and expectation play a part in any audience's experience
> of any performance. There is always an interplay between what
> is actually offered by the artists ... and what the audience brings
> to it.
>
> Jo Salas, 'What is "Good" Playback Theatre?',
> in Fox and Dauber, *Gathering Voices*, 32

Several years have passed since that sun-filled morning when I stood
in the *odeion* at the Asklepieion in Pergamon and asked its purpose.
First, of course, as I took up this question I sought an answer from
scholars of the ancient world, from art, and from archaeology. During
the course of my research into the cult of Asklepios I have become ever
more certain that a dramatic pageant was performed as part of the
healing ritual. The Greeks created a theatre, *odeion*, or another appropriate viewing space as an integral part of the god's sanctuary. For
having seen an enactment of a healing ritual – the god laying his hands
upon one who needs his aid – the patient's mind would be prepared to
receive the dreams sent by the healing god. The vision experienced in
the *abaton* was prompted by a dramatic performance viewed before
retiring to its chambers. The cures Asklepios provided through
dreams began with dramas performed in the viewing spaces of his
sanctuaries.

I then turned to contemporary literature on how we heal. I found
that many doctors have turned away from the machine-first approach
to finding a cure; they have looked back to the ancient world and seen
that the relationship between doctor and patient, the verbal interaction and the expression of genuine concern suggested by Hippokrates,
is still important. Study after study showed that the 'placebo effect'
can offer healing, often when traditional medicines fail. The patient
trusted the doctor to cure an illness and that trust set the patient on
the road to health. Contemporary studies also show that the power of

belief, such as that brought to the ancient Asklepieion or sites such as Lourdes or Santiago de Compostela, also plays a role in the healing process. The journey itself, the pageantry of the sanctuary's personnel, and the atmosphere of faith and exultation lifted the participant's spirits. The positive emotions thus generated strengthened the body as well. Furthermore, anthropological studies of 'traditional societies' show how drama has played a consistent part in fighting disease. The community's shaman fought against the demons who invaded a patient and the conquest of the demon initiated a cure.

My involvement in the Arts-in-Medicine program at Shands Hospital at the University of Florida provided the final step in my quest to discover the relationship between drama and healing. From standing by as a scholarly observer to active participation as an improv actress in Playback Theatre, I have seen how patients' emotions are uplifted when they see their stories performed, when they hear their concerns given dramatic expression. The mini-dramas enacted by a patient's bedside or in a community space do more than distract; they open for the patients a wide realm of possibilities. As their spirits are lifted, so are their pains, and they can take the first steps toward overcoming their illness and, in time, their disease.

The evidence from the ancient texts and sites, the information gleaned from placebo and anthropological studies, the results seen during my own experiences as an actress at a patient's bedside flow together to show that drama and healing can act together. In the sanctuaries of Asklepios and the contemporary hospital a patient can start on the path to healing after seeing a dramatic enactment of that possibility. In summation, for both hospital patient and theatre audience the catharsis Aristotle described as arising from drama can assist an individual fighting illness. Drama offers the possibility of cure.

A Personal Epilogue

Playback can be appreciated for the fullness of its approach to communication, which will often provide the *conditions* necessary to find a truly enduring answer.

Jonathan Fox, 'A Ritual for our Time',
in Fox and Dauber, *Gathering Voices*, 120

Throughout this book I have written about my experiences acting at a patient's bedside, how I have seen spirits lifted as I enact a story through the forms of Playback Theatre. But my experiences have not been limited to those of performance. During the time I have been working on this project I have been in Shands Hospital several times as a patient and during my stay the members of A.I.M. have come to my room. Shortly after beginning my study, I underwent spinal reconstruction surgery and was in Shands hospital for one week. During that time members of the A.I.M. program visited me. One brought paper and tools for me to draw and paste, another did a beautiful dance at my bedside. It was a deeply moving experience. While our musician played her harp, an A.I.M. member gave me a 'guided imagery', guiding my thoughts up Mt Lykabettos, site of my daily walk when I was teaching one summer in Athens. I returned to her words frequently as I lay abed.

While I was writing professional papers on this topic, three times I returned to Shands, twice for surgery, once to monitor a pulmonary embolism. Again members of A.I.M. came to my bedside. They had made a beautiful poster of flowers and love to hang by my bed; Paula Patterson and others enacted scenes of doctors in action, scenes that were both moving and humorous.

During the completion of this book I was diagnosed with cancer and returned to hospital once again for surgery. With this diagnosis I was both mentally and physically exhausted, although I went with a confidence of success born of the many books and studies I had read about the importance of attitude when disease strikes. Once again *Reflections* came to my bedside and through mini-dramas both serious and humorous the actors helped me face both my physical and mental issues. When they left my spirits were lifted and I could better deal with the discomfort of mind and body.

I had long watched the people of A.I.M. in their interaction with patients, at bedside or gathered in a public space, and borne witness to the effect their work has on the hospital residents. But now I can testify as to how their gifts helped my own recoveries. Their words and actions offered a visual reminder of the world outside, a way to direct one's thoughts to happier times. Their enactment of how one can conquer illness and look to health lifted my spirits and aided my return to strength. I close this book by confirming that an Arts-in-

102

V. Conclusion and Epilogue

Medicine program can play a significant role in the healing process, that drama belongs in the contemporary hospital. The ancients recognized this, too, when they built theatres in the sanctuaries to Asklepios.

Notes

I. Drama and Healing in Contemporary Medicine

1. The 1998 movie based on Hunter 'Patch' Adams' book, *Gesundheit: Good Health is a Laughing Matter*, screenplay by Steve Oedekerk, starred Robin Williams as the zany but brilliant doctor. In real life Hunter Campbell 'Patch' Adams, M.D. (1945-) is a physician, social activist, and professional clown. In 1972 he founded the *Gesundheit! Institute*, where he promotes a different health care model, one which teaches that a person's health is connected to that of his family and community. Adams urges his medical students to treat their patients with compassion and use both humour and play to aid their healing.

2. Graham-Pole *et al.* (1994): 19; Patch Adams' introduction to Graham-Pole (2000): iii.

3. The succinct quotation comes from Jay Quinlan "Psychoneuroimmunology", http://www.nfnlp.com/psychoneuroimmunology_quinlan.htm. More technical explanations can be found, for example, in Song and Leonard (2000).

4. Ader and Cohen (1991[2]). In a brief history of the subject, Ader writes (1996: 1), 'Psychoneuroimmunology refers to the study of the interactions among behavioral, neural and endocrine (or neuroendocrine) and immunological processes of adaptation ... The term was first used in 1980, in my presidential address to the American Psychosomatic Society.'

5. Pert (1997) sets out her discoveries enthusiastically in a first-person narrative of her work; it is a book that reads more like a novel than a scientific study. Her research is sound, however, and her science good. For a summary see Quinlan (n. 3): Pert's work showed that

> Neuropeptides are present on both the cell walls of the brain and in the immune system ... The centre for the brain that deals with emotional issues is the limbic system and in particular the hypothalamus ... Showing that the immune and endocrine systems are modulated not only by the brain but by the central nervous system itself has had an impact on how we see disease and how it is created.

A clear summary of Pert's work and the action of peptides may also be found in Hafen *et al.* (1996): 30-1.

6. See Martin (1997). Martin's book is a well-documented account of the interrelationship between the brain and healing.

7. Song and Leonard define their terms: 'In the Hygeian school of Greek

medicine, based on the teachings of Hippocrates, health was viewed as the natural state of the body.' They continue, 'The Asclepian school of medicine, based on the physician Asclepius ... has profoundly influenced modern medicine by focusing on diseases, their causes and cures.'

8. Talbot (2000): 44. A full discussion with numerous examples illustrating the power of hope to heal may be found in Hafen *et al.* (1996): 443-61.

9. Talbot (2000): 44. The information in Talbot's article is frequently cited as a key study of the placebo effect as understood in the popular media in recent years. Dr Mosely's work was reported at msnbc.com/news (July 2002). His study shows clearly that the belief the arthroscopic surgery had been done was as effective as the actual procedure.

10. In addition to Spiro (1986) and Brody (2000), see the many examples in Hafen *et al.* (1996), especially 429-40, Shapiro (1997) and Peters (2001).

11. As reported on NBC (and other stations) nightly news; my quotation comes from msnbc.com/news. The study, which appeared in the *New England Journal of Medicine* in July 2002, is cited by Groopman (2004): 175-7, with information on further fake surgeries performed on patients with ruptured lumbar disks. Again, both those who received actual surgery and those who were merely told the surgery had been performed reported a decrease in pain.

12. Information from ABC News Medical Unit, 24 September 2007, online at http://abcnews.go.com/health. ABC News reported these details:

> Dr Endres and other researchers in Germany compared the effectiveness of acupuncture to conventional treatments. They analyzed over 1,000 patients with chronic lower back pain who received true acupuncture, sham acupuncture or conventional treatments. Randomly assigned patients received two treatments weekly for six months and were then evaluated as to improvement in pain and functional ability. Almost half of the patients in both acupuncture groups benefited from the study, reporting at least a 30 percent decrease in pain or 12 percent improvement in functional ability. In contrast, only one fourth of the patients in the conventional therapy group reported an improvement.

13. As quoted in Hafen *et al.* (1996): 377. Siegel is frequently quoted in Hafen; his own story may be read in Siegel (1989).

14. The term used by Levin (2001). Levin's extensive research seems to show that persons with more active religious participation have better health. The positive results may very well lie, he agrees, on the fact that all religions set out guidelines of appropriate behaviour to promote a long and productive life in harmony with nature and nature's laws; those who actively follow these guidelines have adopted a healthy life style based on the depth of their belief.

15. I discuss the origin of this misplaced symbol below in Chapter II.1: The God.

16. This distinction between healing and cures, common to all studies, is clearly set out by Strathern and Stewart (1999: 7):

As we, and other medical anthropologists use the term, curing refers to an act of treating successfully a specific condition, for example a wound or infestation by worms. Healing, by contrast, refers to the whole person or the whole body seen as an integrated system with both physical and spiritual components. Bio-medicine, in this view, deals with curing and not healing; alternative medicine and the medical systems of various cultures may depend on a philosophy of healing that either encompasses or stands outside of curing.

17. The ancient patients were able to recall their dreams and the procedures they experienced in the *abaton*. The modern surgical patient is given drugs so that what happened in the O.R. cannot be remembered; amnesia is deliberately induced.

18. For a full discussion of diagnosis and dreams, see Oberhelman (1987) *passim*.

19. Shakespeare, *As You Like It* Act 2; the same phrase may be found in the *Palatine Anthology* IX.72 attributed to Palladas.

II. Drama and Healing in Ancient Greece

1. Asklepios is not alone in being rescued from a pyre: Dionysos, too, was snatched from the destroyed body of his mother Semele by Zeus. But the King of the Gods sewed the babe into his own thigh for a later (although equally odd) birth.

2. It is worth noting that Cheiron, in addition to educating Asklepios, to whom he taught the skills of medicine, also instructed Jason and Achilles. Just why the Greeks posited that their heroes gained their education from the bizarre man-horse centaur is an interesting question I cannot pursue here.

3. A good basic summary of the 'life' of Asklepios can be found in Walton (1894, repr. 1979). The Edelsteins offer a full account and the sources from which it develops.

4. Which heroic man was raised differs according to the teller; the list of the restored includes Hippolytos, Capaneus, Tyndareos, Hymenaeus and Glaucus.

5. Pindar, however, gives a very different account in *Pythian* III.8-46, claiming it was Asklepios' desire for money that drove him to go so far in his healing. Diodorus *Bibliotheca Historica* IV.71: 1-4 (Edelstein T-4) denies the god resurrected the dead, preferring to say that Asklepios cured those so near death that it seemed he had revived someone already dead.

6. A detail pointed out by Edelsteins (II.217); they claim that Herakles also is never shown without a robe (*chitôn*). One must remember, however, that this is the Greek custom; the Romans had no problem with showing

Herakles nude (see the Farnese Hercules). The post-classical world often portrayed Asklepios unclothed as well: a statue of the god by Niccolo Tribolo, now in the Boboli Gardens in Florence, deliberately breaks from the ancient tradition by showing Asklepios naked. See Schouten (1967): 184.

7. The Edelsteins (II.227) cite Festus *De Verborum Significatu* 110 (T-691) and Eusebius *Praeparatio Evangelica* III.11.26 (T-706).

8. In addition to Schouten (1967): 117-32, see also Blayney, 'Caduceus vs the Staff of Asclepius (Asklepian)', online at www.drblayney.com/Asclepius.html.

9. One exception to this requirement exists on the *iamata* (IG IV^2 1 Stele B.xxv = Edelstein T-423.25). Sostrata of Pherae was suffering from worms. She went to Epidauros and slept there, but having had no clear dream she let herself be carried home. On the way a 'man of fine appearance' came to her, cut her open and took out the worms. Having made her well, 'Asklepios' revealed his presence and asked that she send a thank-offering to Epidauros. Thus her story was recorded on the sanctuary stelae.

10. Aleshire (1989: 103-10 and 1992: 92-8) discusses the topic and describes the 'life history' of the offerings.

11. Livy 10.47 records the Senate's decision to bring the snake; Ovid (*Metamorphoses* 15.622-744) reports how the sacred snake, brought up the Tiber to Rome, of its own free will chose residence on the Isola Tiberina. A temple to the healing god was dedicated there on 1 January 291 BC and its archaeological evidence has recently been verified. Today a hospital of the Fatebenefratelli stands on Tiber Island, and the church of San Bartolomeo occupies the site of Asklepios' temple. The island's shape is said to be that of a ship with the sacred snake carved upon it in relief. And a performance space was available nearby, for Pompey's theatre stands just across the Tiber.

12. The relief is *IG* II^2 4359. Aleshire (1989: 94) discredits the idea that these are physicians, concluding that 'it is probable that the five honorands were crowned for activities in connection with the cult of Asklepios, perhaps in connection with the establishment of state control over the cult, rather than for any service as public physicians'. My interpretation avoids the difficulties of the issue.

13. Bad dreams were considered to be omens that prompted sacrifices: Artemidorus reports (*Oneirocritica* V.66 = Edelstein T-454) that when a man dreamed he should pray to Asklepios and he did not, his hand was crushed in an accident the next day. Thus he knew he should perform 'averting sacrifices' to the god – *thuein apotropaia tôi theôi*.

14. As documented by Aleshire (1989: 42). Eye complaints are documented as common in remote communities today. For example, in recent years public attention has been focused on how blindness is a serious public health problem in Tibet, with prevalence higher than in similar studies in eastern China. Medical groups that have started clinics in the area report that about 75% of blindness in Tibet can be either prevented or treated. See (among others)

Gaynor *et al.*, 'Eliminating Trachoma in Areas with Limited Disease', *Emerging Infectious Diseases* 2003: 9(5): 596-8, online at http://www.medscape.com/viewarticle/457184_4

15. In historical times, according to some accounts, Athens suffered a plague in the 630s as a result of the Cylonian affair and subsequent murders. The plague, the Cylonian affair and the *kathartai* called in to cleanse the city (in particular, one Epimenides from Crete) are discussed by Gorrini (2005: 135-8). There is considerable scholarly doubt about Epimenides and the actions of these *kathartai*.

16. Teijeiro (1993: 124-5) continues, explaining the difference between magic and religion:

> When one prays to a god, one asks for something which depends on his will and which can be graciously conceded; when a magic rite is performed, one demands of the power invoked that it acts in a certain manner. Religion, moreover, is much more than the act of prayer and supplication, since it touches on all the fundamental aspects of human life; magic in contrast, deals with specific issues and tries to satisfy the magician's or his client's specific desires.

17. Of the many good descriptions of the archaeological site of Epidauros, one of the best is that by Tomlinson (1983). Much of the information here is taken from his book. I focus on the major structures of the sanctuary and have not repeated here his discussion of the buildings whose identification is uncertain or of those structures to divinities and heroes who did not play a central role in the healing process. Details about the temple itself come from Burford (1969).

18. Pausanias (V.11.11) says that when at Epidauros he asked why neither oil nor water was poured for the god, he was told it was because Asklepios' statue stood atop a well. Levi's note (230: 107) says that this was in the *tholos* at Epidauros.

19. Tomlinson (1983) 82-4 suggests the use of this Romanized redesign was related to ritual dramas.

20. Tomlinson (1992: 114) asserts that the altar is 'almost certainly the "Satan's Seat" of the *Book of Revelation* (2.13)'.

21. Certainly the sanctuary of the god on Tiber Island in Rome is equally famous (see Ch. II, n. 11 above).

22. Information on the Corinthian Asklepieion is taken from Lang (1977).

23. The layout of the Greek sacred areas was identified by Doxiades in 1937; Stillwell (1954) has confirmed his work. The placement of the temple within its sacred area (*temenos*) is such that the first view offered the spectator is oblique; the Greeks, unlike the Romans, did not favour axial symmetry. Doxiades (1972) developed his ideas further, suggesting that certain angles of vision were related to whether the building was in the Doric or Ionic order.

24. This and following information is from Pandermalis (1997).

25. See the report of Orlandos' work in Habicht (1985): 40-4.

26 . Site information for Oropos is taken from Petracos (1995) and Coulton (1968).

27. Semeria (1986) carried out a thorough and careful study of Asklepieia around the Greek world. I am completely indebted to her scholarly work on the existence and location of the healing sanctuaries for the information here. Her study gives the archaeological and epigraphical evidence, as well as a listing of the artifacts relating to the cult of Asklepios found on each site.

28. Semeria (1986) links theatre and Asklepieion. Levi (1971) notes in his translation (p.161 n.79) that the theatre was identified in 1924, and adds that the church of Panagia Rachiotissa 'consists almost entirely of classical stones and probably stands in Demeter's enclosure.'

29. Aleshire (1991: 39): '*The paianistai* listed on *IG* II^2 2481 form a larger and perhaps more nearly complete choir, with a membership of at least 29, of whom 9 held the *civitas* and 16 were citizens of Athens. None of these men are known to have had other associations with the cult of Asklepios, but those from whom prosopographic connections can be traced clearly belong ... to the higher levels of Athenian social and economic life.' The fact that their names are listed at the sanctuary, however, seems to indicate to me that they were, indeed, associated with the god.

30. Wells (1998: 42 n. 302) quotes scholars who have so suggested, but opts for Aleshire's explanations as more tenable: such small dedications could easily have been lost or 'that visual problems were for some reason especially prevalent in Athens ca. 250 BC'; see Aleshire (1989): 42.

III. Drama and Healing in the
Contemporary American Hospital

1. The Homeric bard composed orally; he had certain stock phrases, *formulae*, which helped him to complete a line metrically or describe a common recurring scene. Lord (2000) is the basic text on Homeric oral composition.

2. Information on Moreno cited from Schattner and Courtney (eds) (1981): 7.

3. Susan Massad (2003) *Advances in Mind-Body Medicine*. The quotation here comes from Lewis (2003). I have discussed Dr Massad's work with her on several occasions.

4. Paula Patterson is a trained drama therapist who has completed the program for teaching Playback Theatre. With a background in theatre and nursing in addition to her therapy training, she brings to the drama troupe a wide expertise.

5. Richard A. Lippin, foreword to Malchiodi (1999): 10.

6. Simon (1978: 87-8) writes these words in relation to those suffering mental illness – he is a psychiatrist. He sees implications from the 'Homeric model of mind', as he terms it, for the contemporary models of mental illness. He concludes his argument (88), 'In sum, modes of mind and mental illness

contain certain presuppositions about the individual and the collective, and these presuppositions are operative in the "group" that consists of the healer and the patient.'

7. 'Pathography' refers to the recent genre of literature in which a patient writes of his/her battle against a disease. Usually the book reports a successful outcome, but some pathographies remain as a last testament to a person's emotions during the final hours of life.

8. Salas (1996[2]: 111-2) lists the three categories of the assault on the identity, the need for respect, and the aesthetic importance of the experience, when 'life is distilled into art'.

9. Drama is also used at the University of Florida's College of Medicine in the Standardized Patient Program. Dr George T. Harrell, founding dean of the University's College of Medicine, established the Harrell Center to help train would-be doctors in successful evaluation and treatment of patients.

In this program volunteers are trained to enact signs and symptoms of specific ailments. Medical students or residents interact with the actor, the 'standardized patient', by taking a history, performing a physical examination, or suggesting a treatment plan. This encounter is monitored by video camera and/or observed through a one-way window; doctors later review the scene with the students. I have acted in the Harrell Program as a standardized patient, and I hope some of my comments have helped the young medical students to communicate better with their real patients. Some of the would-be doctors clearly show they understand the importance of empathy; others need to learn they are facing real people, not merely an example of a specific disease.

10. This performance has been captured on the DVD produced (2006) by Hemal Trivedi of our work, 'Acting Healthy: Playback Theatre in a Medical Hospital'.

IV. Asklepios Beyond the Classical World

1. By the Byzantine period, however, Christ becomes Christ Pantokrator; the face looking down from the dome at Daphne, for example, does not show a compassionate God.

2. See Edelsteins II: 130-1; they add, 'Asclepius led [men] to immortality and to the true life, just as Christ promised to do for his adherents.' Their discussion (II.132-8) of Asklepios and Christ offers much food for thought and shows in detail how the two are alike and how they differ.

3. Temkin continues (1991: 98-100) that it is difficult to determine whether Jesus healed through the human emotion of pity, a sense of mission 'or the need for legitimization'. He adds also that Jesus threw out demons but that Asklepios did not seem to have worried about such creatures.

4. One of the changes in Christian healing beliefs was that, in time, the

relics of saints were believed to have the power to cure. For a discussion on this development, see Dawson (1935): 159-71.

5. For example, both Madrid and Munich claim to possess both skulls. There are also discrepancies about which days are sacred to the saints: the Catholic Church celebrates them on 27 September while the Orthodox Churches honour Kosmas and Damian on three dates: 1 July, 17 October, and 1 November.

6. Sometimes other ancient deities were replaced by healing saints as well. For example, in Rome Pope Felix IV redesigned the Library of Peace into the Basilica of Santi Cosma e Damiano, where it backs onto the old monument of Romulus.

Select Bibliography

While most of the books and articles listed here are cited within the body or notes of the text, I have included other references as well. The latter are here first because the ideas they express form part of my thinking even though I do not give direct quotations from them. For instance, Bernard Lown's *The Lost Art of Healing* is a fine book I read early on in my study and his ideas directed me to some of the other books that discuss the role of doctor and patient. For the ancient world, for example, Dillon's excellent *Pilgrims and Pilgrimage in Ancient Greece* gave me background for my reading on pilgrims to holy sites in the modern world. For an understanding of the archaeology of the south slope of the Acropolis in Athens, John Freeley's *Strolling Through Athens* is a fine guide and one I used on several occasions when walking the area. Secondly, I thought that readers of my book might like to look at some of these non-cited studies on their own.

1. The ancient world

Aleshire, Sara B. (1989) *The Athenian Asklepieion: The People, Their Dedications, and the Inventories* (Amsterdam).

Aleshire, Sara B. (1991) *Asklepios at Athens: Epigraphic and Prosopographic Essays on the Athenian Healing Cults* (Amsterdam).

Aleshire, Sara B. (1992) 'The Economics of Dedication at the Athenian Asklepieion', in Tullia Linders and Brita Alroth (eds) *Economics of Cult in the Ancient Greek World* (Uppsala): 85-98.

Behr, Charles A. (1968) *Aelius Aristides and the Sacred Tales* (Amsterdam).

Bonuzzi, Luciano (1992) 'Angoscia e malattia nei santuari di Asclepio e alle origini del pellegrinaggio cristiano', in Antje Krug (ed.) *From Epidauros to Salerno* (Leiden): 51-9.

Bowman, John (1992) *Kos: General Guide* (Athens).

Bremer, J.M. (1981) 'Greek Hymns', in H.S. Versnel (ed.) *Faith, Hope and Worship. Aspects of Religious Mentality in the Ancient World.* (Leiden): 193-215.

Burford, Alison (1969) *Greek Temple Builders at Epidauros* (Liverpool and Toronto).

Burkert, Walter (1985) *Greek Religion*, translated by John Raffan (Cambridge, MA).

Cohn-Haft, L. (1956) *The Public Physicians of Ancient Greece* (Northampton, MA).

113

Cook, Robert and Kathleen (1968) *Southern Greece: An Archaeological Guide* (New York).

Coulton, James J. (1968) 'The Stoa at the Amphiareion, Oropos', *Annual of the British School at Athens* 63: 147-83.

Devereux, George (1976) *Dreams in Greek Tragedy: An Ethno-Psycho-Analytical Study* (Berkeley and Los Angeles).

Dillon, Matthew (1994) 'The Didactic Nature of the Epidaurian Iamata', *Zeitschrift für Papyrologie und Epigraphik* 101: 239-60.

Dillon, Matthew (1997) *Pilgrims and Pilgrimage in Ancient Greece* (London and New York).

Dodds, E.R. (1951) *The Greeks and the Irrational* (Berkeley).

Doxiades, C.A. (1972) *Architectural Space in Ancient Greece* (Cambridge).

Easterling, P.E. and J.V. Muir (eds) (1985) *Greek Religion and Society.* (Cambridge).

Edelstein, Ludwig and Emma J. (1998 [1945]) *Asclepius: A Collection and Interpretation of the Testimonies*, vols I and II (Baltimore).

Festugière, A.J. (1960) *Personal Religion Among the Greeks* (Berkeley).

Frantz, Alison (1975) 'Pagan Philosophers in Christian Athens', *Proceedings of the American Philosophical Society* 119: 29-38.

Freely, John (1991) *Strolling Through Athens* (London).

Garland, Robert (1992) *Introducing New Gods: Politics of Athenian Religion* (London).

Gorrini, Maria Elena (2005) 'The Hippocratic Impact on Healing Cults: The Archaeological Evidence in Attica', in Philip J. Van Der Eijk (ed.) *Hippocrates in Context* (Leiden): 135-56.

Gourevitch, Danielle (1984) *Le Triangle Hippocratique dans le Monde Gréco-Romain: Le Malade, sa Maladie et son Médecin* (Paris and Rome).

Habicht, Christian (1985) *Pausanias' Guide to Ancient Greece* (Berkeley).

Halliwell, Stephen (1997) *Aristophanes: Birds, Lysistrata, Assembly-Women, Wealth*, translated with introduction and notes (Oxford).

Hammarskjöld, Dag (1964) *Markings* (New York).

Hartigan, Karelisa (2005) 'Drama and Healing: Ancient and Modern', in Helen King (ed.) *Health in Antiquity* (London): 162-79.

Holowchak, M. Andrew (2002) *Ancient Science and Dreams: Oneirology in Greco-Roman Antiquity* (Lanham).

Horstmanshoff, H.F.J. (2004) 'Asclepius and Temple Medicine in Aelius Aristides' *Sacred Tales*', in *Magic and Rationality in Ancient Near Eastern and Graeco-Roman Medicine* (Leiden): 325-41.

Jackson, Ralph (1988) *Doctors and Diseases in the Roman Empire* (London).

Jones, C.P. (1998) 'Aelius Aristides and the Asclepieion', in Helmut Koester (ed.) *Pergamon, Citadel of the Gods: Archaeological Record, Literary Description and Religious Development* (Harrisburg): 63-76.

King, Helen (ed.) (2005) *Health in Antiquity* (London).

Krug, Antje (1992) 'Archive in Heiligtümern', in Antje Krug (ed.) *From Epidauros to Salerno* (Leiden): 187-200.

Select Bibliography

Lang, Mabel (1977) *Cure and Cult in Ancient Corinth* (Princeton).

Levi, Peter (tr.) (1971) *Pausanias: Guide to Greece*, vol. I: *Central Greece*; vol. II: *Southern Greece* (Penguin).

Li Donnici, Lynn R. (1995) *The Epidaurian Miracles Inscriptions: Text, Translation and Commentary* (Atlanta).

Linders, Tullia (1990) 'Sacred Finances: Some Observations', in Tullia Linders (ed.) *Economics of Cult in the Ancient Greek World* (Uppsala): 9-14.

Lloyd, G.E.R. (ed.) (1978) *Hippocratic Writings* (Harmondsworth).

Lord, Albert B. (2000) *The Singer of Tales*[2] ed. Stephen Mitchell and Gregory Nagy (with CD Rom) (Harvard).

Marinatos, Nanno and Robin Hägg (1993) *Greek Sanctuaries: New Approaches* (London and New York).

McLeish, Kenneth and J. Michael Walton (1994) *Aristophanes: Ploutos/ Wealth*, translation and introduction (London).

Meier, C.A. (1967) *Ancient Incubation and Modern Psychotherapy*, tr. Monica Curtis (Evanston).

Mikalson, Jon (1975) *The Sacred and Civil Calendar of the Athenian Year* (Princeton).

Oberhelman, Steven M. (1981) 'The Interpretation of Prescriptive Dreams in Ancient Greek Medicine', *Journal of the History of Medicine and Allied Sciences* 36:4: 416-24.

Oberhelman, Steven M. (1987) 'The Diagnostic Dream in Ancient Medical Theory and Practice', *Bulletin of the History of Medicine* 61-1: 47-60.

Oliver, James H. (1935) 'The Sarapion Monument and the Paean of Sophocles', *Hesperia* 5: 91-122.

Padel, Ruth (1994) *In and Out of the Mind: Greek Images of the Tragic Self* (Princeton).

Pandermalis, D. (1997) *Dion, The Archaeological Site and the Museum* [site guide] (Athens).

Petracos, Basil Chr. (1995) *The Amphiareion of Oropos* [site guide] (Athens).

Phillips, E.D. (1987) *Aspects of Greek Medicine* (Philadelphia).

Risse, Guenter B. (1999) *Mending Bodies, Saving Souls: A History of Hospitals* (New York).

Schlaifer, Robert (1940) 'Notes on Athenian Public Cults', *Harvard Studies in Classical Philology* 51: 233-60.

Schouten, J. (1967) *The Rod and Serpent of Asklepios: Symbol of Medicine* (Amsterdam).

Semeria, Alessandra (1986) 'Per un Censimento degli Asklepeia della Grecia Continentale e delle Isole', *Annali della Scuola Normale Superiori di Pisa* 16: 931-58.

Simon, Bennett (1978) *Mind and Madness in Ancient Greece: The Classical Roots of Modern Psychiatry* (Ithaca, NY).

Stillwell, Richard (1954) 'The Siting of Classical Greek Temples', *Journal of the Society of Architectural Historians* XIII: 3-8.

Stillwell, Richard, ed. (1976) *Princeton Encyclopedia of Classical Sites* (Princeton).

Teijeiro, M. Garcia (1993) 'Religion and Magic', *Kernos* 6: 123-38.

Temkin, Owsei (1977) *The Double Face of Janus and Other Essays in the History of Medicine* (Baltimore).

Temkin, Owsei (1991) *Hippocrates in a World of Pagans and Christians* (Baltimore)

Tomlinson, Richard (1983) *Epidauros: An Archaeological Guide* (Austin).

Tomlinson, Richard (1992) *From Mycenae to Constantinople: The Evolution of the Ancient City* (London and New York).

Van der Eijk, Philip J. (1990) 'The "Theology" of the Hippocratic Treatise *On the Sacred Disease*', *Apeiron* 23: 87-119.

Versnel, H.S. (ed.) (1981) *Faith, Hope and Worship: Aspects of Religious Mentality in the Ancient World* (Leiden).

Wagman, Robert (1995) *Inni di Epidauro* (Pisa).

Walton, Alice (1979) *Asklepios: The Cult of the Greek God of Medicine* (Chicago).

Wells, Louise (1998) *The Greek Language of Healing from Homer to New Testament Times* (Berlin and New York).

Wycherley, R.E. (1978) *The Stones of Athens* (Princeton).

Yenens, S. (1998) *Turkish Odyssey* (Istanbul).

2. Contemporary medicine/ holistic medicine

ABC News Medical Unit, 24 September 2007, online at http://abcnews .go.com/health.

Achterberg, Jeanne (1985) *Imagery in Healing: Shamanism and Modern Medicine* (Boston and London).

Adams, Patch (2000) Introduction to John Graham-Pole, *Illness and the Art of Creative Self-Expression* (Oakland).

Ader, Robert and Nicholas Cohen (1991[2]) *Psychoneuroimmunology* (San Diego).

Ader, Robert (1996) 'Historical Perspectives on Psychoneuroimmunology', in Herman Friedman, Thomas Klein and Andrea Friedman (eds) *Psychoneuroimmunology, Stress, and Infection* (Boca Raton): 1-24.

Berczeller, Peter (1994) *Doctors and Patients* (New York).

Blayney, Keith 'Caduceus vs the Staff of Asclepius (Asklepian)', online at www.drblayney.com/Asclepius.html.

Brody, Howard (2000) *The Placebo Response: How You Can Release the Body's Inner Pharmacy for Better Health* (New York).

Emunah, Renée (1994) *Acting for Real: Drama Therapy, Process, Technique, and Performance* (New York).

Dawson, George G. (1935/1977) *Healing: Pagan and Christian* (London).

Fontana, David and Lucilia Valente (1993) 'Drama Therapy and the Theory of Psychological Reversals', *Arts in Psychotherapy* 20: 133-42.

Fox, Jonathan and Heinrich Dauber (eds) (1999) *Gathering Voices: Essays on Playback Theatre* (New Paltz).

Frank, Arthur (1991/ rev. 2002) *At the Will of the Body: Reflections on Illness* (Boston and New York).

Frank, Jerome and Julia Frank (1991³) *Persuasion and Healing: A Comparative Study of Psychotherapy* (Baltimore).

Friedman, Herman, Thomas Klein and Andrea Friedman (eds) (1996) *Psychoneuroimmunology, Stress, and Infection* (Boca Raton).

Gaynor, B.D, Y. Miao, V. Cevallos et al. (2003), 'Eliminating Trachoma in Areas with Limited Disease', *Emerging Infectious Diseases* 9(5): 596-98, online at http://www.medscape.com/viewarticle/457184_4

Gordon, James S., Dennis Jaffe and David Bresler (eds) (1984) *Mind, Body Health* (New York).

Graham-Pole, John, Mary Rockwood Lane *et al.* (1994) 'Creating an Arts Program in an Academic Medical Setting', *International Journal of Arts Medicine* 3 (2): 17-25.

Graham-Pole, John (2000) *Illness and the Art of Creative Self-Expression* (Oakland).

Groopman, Jerome (2004) *The Anatomy of Hope: How People Prevail in the Face of Illness* (New York).

Hafen, Brent Q., Keith Karren, Kathryn J. Frandsen and N. Lee Smith (eds) (1996) *Mind/Body Health: The Effects of Attitudes, Emotions and Relationships* (Boston).

Hamilton, Mary (1906) *Incubation: The Cure of Disease in Pagan Temples and Christian Churches* (London).

Homan, Sid (1994) 'The "Theatre" in Medicine', *International Journal of Arts Medicine* 3: 26-29.

Katz, Jay (1984) *The Silent World of Doctor and Patient* (Baltimore and London).

Kedem-Tahar, Efrat and Peter Felix-Kellermann (1996) 'Psychodrama and Drama Therapy: A Comparison', *The Arts in Psychotherapy* 23: 27-36.

Kinsley, David (1996) *Health, Healing and Religion: A Cross-Cultural Perspective* (Saddle River).

Landy, Robert J. (1986) *Drama Therapy: Concepts and Practices* (Springfield).

Landy, Robert J. (1997) 'Drama Therapy – The State of the Art', *The Arts in Psychotherapy* 24: 5-15.

Levin, Jeff (2001) *God, Faith, and Health: Exploring the Spirituality-Healing Connection* (New York).

Lewis, Sheldon (2003) 'Take a Bow – and Call me in the Morning', *Spirituality and Health: The Soul/Body Connection* (September-October): 18.

Lown, Bernard (1996) *The Lost Art of Healing: Practicing Compassion in Medicine* (New York).

Lusebrink, Vija (1999) 'Dreamwork and Sandtray Therapy with Mastectomy Patients', in Cathy Malchiodi (ed.) *Medical Art Therapy with Adults* (London and Philadelphia): 87-111.

Malchiodi, Cathy (1993) 'Medical Art Therapy: Contributions to the Field of Arts Medicine', *International Journal of Arts Medicine* 2: 28-31

Malchiodi, Cathy (ed.) (1999) *Medical Art Therapy with Adults* (London and Philadelphia).

Martin, Paul (1997) *The Healing Mind: The Vital Links Between Brain and Behavior, Immunity and Disease* (New York).

Massad, Susan (2003) 'Performance of Doctoring: A Philosophical and Methodological Approach to Medical Conversation', *Advances in Mind-Body Medicine* 19: 6-13.

McNiff, Shaun (1992) *Arts As Medicine: Creating a Therapy of the Imagination* (Boston and London).

Nuland, Sherwin B. (1988) *Doctors: The Biography of Medicine* (New York).

Pelletier, Kenneth R. (1977) *Mind as Healer, Mind as Slayer* (St Lawrence).

Pendzik, Susana (1994) 'The Theatre Stage and the Sacred Space', *Arts in Psychotherapy* 21: 25-35.

Pert, Candace (1997) *Molecules of Emotion: The Science Behind Mind-Body Medicine* (New York).

Peters, David (ed.) (2001) *Understanding the Placebo Effect in Complementary Medicine: Theory, Practice and Research* (Edinburgh).

Quinlan, Jay 'Psychoneuroimmunology', online at http://www.nfnlp.com/psychoneuroimmunology_quinlan.htm.

Runco, Mark A. and Ruth Richards (eds) (1997) *Eminent Creativity, Everyday Creativity, and Health* (Greenwich and London).

Sacks, Oliver (1984) *A Leg to Stand on* (New York).

Salas, Jo (1996²) *Improvising Real Life* (Dubuque).

Salas, Jo (1999) 'What is "Good" Playback Theatre?' in Jonathan Fox and Heinrich Dauber (eds) *Gathering Voices* (New Paltz).

Samuels, Michael and Mary Rockwood Lane (1998) *Creative Healing: How to Heal Yourself by Tapping Your Hidden Creativity* (San Francisco).

Schattner, Gertrud and Richard Courtney (eds) (1981) *Drama in Therapy*, vol. II: *Adults* (New York).

Scheff, T.J. (1979) *Catharsis in Healing, Ritual and Drama* (Berkeley).

Selzer, Richard (1976) *Mortal Lessons: Notes on the Art of Surgery* (New York).

Selzer, Richard (1981), 'The Surgeon as Priest', in Trautman (ed.) (1981).

Selzer, Richard (1987) *Taking the World in for Repair* (London).

Shapiro, Arthur K. (1997) *The Powerful Placebo: From Ancient Priest to Modern Physician* (Baltimore).

Siegel, Bernie (1989) *Peace, Love and Healing: Bodymind Communication and the Path to Self-Healing: An Exploration* (New York).

Song, Cai and Brian E. Leonard (2000) *Fundamentals of Psychoneuroimmunology* (Chichester).

Spiro, Howard M. (1986) *Doctors, Patients, and Placebos* (New Haven).

Stein, Michael (2007) *The Lonely Patient: How We Experience Illness* (New York).

Strathern, Andrew and Pamela J. Stewart (1999) *Curing and Healing: Medical Anthropology in Global Perspective* (Durham, NC).

Talbot, Margaret (2000) 'The Placebo Prescription', *New York Times Magazine* (9 January): 44-7.

Tick, Edward (2001) *The Practice of Dream Healing* (Wheaten).

Trautman, Joanne (ed.) (1981) *Healing Arts in Dialogue: Medicine and Literature* (Carbondale).

Warren, Bernie (ed.) (1984) *Using the Creative Arts in Therapy* (London and Cambridge, MA).

Wright, Stephen G. and Jean Sayre-Adams (2000) *Sacred Space, Right Relationship and Spirituality in Healthcare* (London).

Index

Index